D1056124

Praying the Kings

Mining Old Testament Judges, Kings, and
Unsung Heroes For
Daily Leadership Guidance

John P. Chandler

Illustrated by Jessica Luttrull

Foreword by Alan Hirsch and Mike Breen

Joshua - Esther

Published by *Uptick Imprint,* 4 Lee Court, Lake Monticello, Virginia, 22963, USA.

All Scripture quotations are taken from The New Oxford Annotated Bible containing the Old and New Testaments, edited by Bruce M. Metzger and Roland E. Murphy, New Revised Standard Version, Oxford University Press, New York, NY, 1991, 1994.

Design: Jessica Luttrull
USA ISBN-13: 978-0-9890816-2-7
Printed in the United States of America. First printing, 2013.

Library of Congress Cataloguing-in-Publication Data
Chander, John, 1961-

Praying the Kings: Mining Old Testament Judges, Kings, and Unsung Heroes for Daily Leadership Guidance

ISBN-13: 978-0-9890816-2-7
1. Leadership; 2. Guidance; 3. Discipleship; 4. Old Testament

What others are saying about the "Praying ..." Series

"John's gift of helping leaders look at their role through the lenses of scripture is a gift that is beyond measure. This book is a sacred offering to those who have been called and entrusted to lead. Seasoned leaders and emerging leaders will be inspired to lead others in "the way" that will provide the most significant imprint a leader can leave – the imprint of Christ."

Jan Bazow
Founder and CEO, Fortis Group | Richmond, Virginia

"Some pontificate on leadership without actually getting their hands dirty leading. Some leverage leadership ideals to boost their ego rather than to lay down their life for God's Kingdom. It's rare to find someone who surrenders themselves to the tiresome work of leading with both humility and courage. Even rarer is when this person can also guide us along the same path. John Chandler is one of these rare leaders."

Winn Collier
Author, Holy Curiosity | Pastor, All Souls Charlottesville | Charlottesville, Virginia

"John Chandler is the kind of guy I from which I want to learn about Scripture. He knows and loves the Bible. He understands our world. He studies leadership (and leads well himself). And he cares about people. Working through the reflections, I've seen first-hand how John's combination of scholarship and experience makes "Praying" simple

but not simplistic, scholarly but not pedantic, and inspirational but not sappy."

Travis Collins
Author, Tough Calls | Pastor, Bon Air Baptist Church | Richmond, Virginia

"John Chandler is a follower of Jesus who will captivate you as he takes you on a personal journey through God's word. He will challenge your thinking and call you to act on the same verses that led to the God stories we all love! As someone who has had the privilege of being before Kings, there is no experience greater than being in the presence of the King of Kings. John is a personal friend and a leader who demonstrates Christ-like love. I know he will inspire you as he has me, to live out God's word."

Jimmie Davidson
PEACE Pastor, Saddleback Church, California | Founding Pastor of Highlands Fellowship, Abingdon, Virginia

"There is no compromise for principle-based leadership and John's "Praying" books are extraordinarily inspiring. These books give each of us insight which can be applied not only to our roles as leaders, but also importantly, who we are as followers. John is truly one of our most prized thought leaders and I am left inspired following every interaction I have with him. These are books I will keep at my side and recommend to all who humbly strive to lead and follow as God would have us do."

Tiffany Franks
President of Averett University | Danville, Virginia

"Working with college students, I know the importance of quick and memorable coffee house communication. Jessica Luttrull has an artist's knack for communicating complex concepts in ways that are catchy, memorable, and even profound. Pair that with John Chandler's concise discoveries of biblical wisdom and you get an elegant, potent, and useful daily handbook for growing as a biblical leader."

Evan Hansen
Director of Eunoia | www.beautifulthinking.org | Charlottesville, Virginia

"John Chandler has shaped countless ministers through his tireless commitment leadership development. I am blessed to be one of them. As a leader of leaders, many of whom have no formal biblical training, I am grateful for this leadership development tool. John has made biblical wisdom accessible, impactful and memorable for Christians at all levels of leadership and all stages of spiritual maturity. Visual learners like me will love the drawings that anyone can replicate as they share these nuggets of wisdom with others."

Wendy McCaig
Author, From the Sanctuary to the Streets | Founder and Executive Director, Embrace Richmond | Richmond, Virginia

"I have been studying the Bible now for over six decades, and I am continually amazed at the fresh insights God provides me each time I open His book. In his "Praying" books, my good friend John Chandler also provides some fresh, practical insights into how to make your Bible study more productive and how to become a better leader in the process.

Focusing on the Old Testament, particularly the rich history of Israel and its kings and leaders, John reviews a chapter, highlights a truth and then makes a practical application.

Read this book because it's witty, insightful, and practical, but also read this book because it is written by a proven leader who knows what he is talking about, who has dealt with the enormous challenges of training young ministers to be more effective in advancing the kingdom in a culture that, morally, looks very similar to Israel during the reign of its kings and leaders over 3000 years ago.

John's leadership of Spence Network has transformed the lives of many young ministers and better prepared them to take on the challenges of leading the church in the 21st Century. I have seen the result of John's work first hand in the transformed lives of many young leaders he has invested in; his book may transform your life as well."

Bob Russell
Author, When God Builds a Church | Bob Russell Ministries |
Louisville, Kentucky

"The power of the Baptist movement in history is its belief that any person has access to the heart of God through Jesus Christ. When we humbly submit ourselves to the Bible and see ourselves reflected there, we can trust that the Holy Spirit will speak to us, and that we can hear, respond, and lead. This is one reason I am excited that my friend and fellow leader John Chandler has written these leadership devotionals. These reflections are both suitable for presidents, and for ordinary folk on church nominating committees. They will help anyone who wants to lead biblically and lead well. It is my hope that every Baptist in Virginia *and around the world who has to make decisions will use John's book to turn their hearts to the God of the Bible who can give wisdom for daily leading. Trust me, you will be changed and you will be a better leader!"*

John Upton
Executive Director, Baptist General Association of Virginia | President, Baptist World Alliance | Richmond and Falls Church, Virginia

"Great Bible exegesis is only truly great when it spans the millennia to inform and inspire our world today. John Chandler has that unique ability to interpret scripture with integrity and application. Moreover John's own walk with Jesus matches the words he brings to print. I thoroughly commend John's writings to anyone looking to strengthen their walk with Jesus.

Craig Vernall
National Leader. Baptist Churches of New Zealand | Tauranga, New Zealand

"John Chandler has provided a key ingredient in the formation of any effective congregational leader: regular, consistent, insightful and inspiring study of scripture. His insights are simple, yet profound. His approach is extremely user-friendly and accessible. His knowledge of congregational life is not naïve or divorced from reality. I am grateful for this powerful addition to our efforts to raise up leaders for God's people in the 21st century."

Bill Wilson
President, Center for Congregational Health | Winston-Salem, North Carolina

Dedication

For my home church, Friendly Avenue Baptist in Greensboro, North Carolina, for teaching me to love the Bible, and for ordaining me to spread the Good News;

and for all of the Virginia Baptist churches where I've had the joy of serving: Effort, University, Mt. Shiloh, Fork Union, Chestnut Grove, Spring Hill, and All Souls Charlottesville;

Thank you for demonstrating what the Bible looks like in human form through Holy Spirit-led community.

Table of Contents

Foreword to the "Praying" series

By Alan Hirsch and Mike Breen

Those who would reactivate the missional church must first awaken a missional form of discipleship. Clearly, it will take the whole people of God – apostles, prophets, evangelists, pastors, and teachers – to catalyze a movement of the Kingdom of God in the West. We are long past the day of believing that this movement can rest alone in the hands of superstar preachers and celebrity Christians. Every revolution is led by an uprising of peasants, not the edict of kings. And the revolution of Jesus' Kingdom breaking in on earth as it is in heaven is no different. It will take place when ordinary disciples lead the church in the world.

But where are all of these ordinary apostles, prophets, evangelists, shepherds, and teachers going to come from? From disciples who are becoming more acculturated to the ways of Jesus than tamed by pervasive cultural mores. And they are going to become acculturated to Jesus' forgotten ways by learning a rhythm of daily engagement with his presence.

The early church exploded from a minor sect to a world movement when it embraced an "all-hands-on-deck" missional form of living and leading – that is, when every follower of Jesus did the heavy lifting. Ordinary people had to act as apostles, prophets, evangelists, shepherds, and teachers. No one sat on their hands and waited for the twelve famous people who walked with Jesus to do all of the leading. And if we want to see the West today transformed

John P. Chandler 1

from dying Christendom to a reawakened missional movement of the Kingdom of God, then it will take all of us being better leaders. The only way we become better leaders is by becoming better followers, better listeners. We are all going to have to embrace a spirituality that learns to listen to and follow the God of the Bible.

If you want to sit around at Sunday lunch and argue that if your preacher would only preach a little better, then all would be well, you are sadly mistaken. Sure, better preaching is helpful. But alone, your pastor is not enough, and preaching is clearly not enough. It will barely budge the church, let alone the neighborhood – or the world, for heaven's sake! It doesn't all depend on platform people. It depends on all of us being disciples, and on disciples being leaders.

This is why I am so excited about John Chandler's series of books that demonstrate a path for praying through the Bible. Even better, these are excellent, mature, articulate, and distinctly *adult* types of reflection. There is a scholarly depth and social breadth beneath the concise and understandable applications of Scripture. But though academically and theologically sound (and at times profound), what we come out with when we read these reflections is *clarity*. Things are clear enough that I can scribble them down on a napkin and show you something that might inform a decision you have to make that day. We learn to listen to the Bible with the full expectation that God will speak to us. And as God speaks to us and leads us, we become more capable of leading others as well.

The "*Praying*" books have credibility because they already have had impact on groups of young adult leaders that John leads called "*Uptick*." It is part of the training: they learn from John how to engage with the Bible and catch the rhythm of discipleship, learn to live dynamically engaging God's Kingdom in the world. This in turn has been part of reshaping his tribe, Virginia Baptists, into one of the most refreshing and innovative denominations I have experienced in the last few years. As James Davison Hunter has written, movements that "change the world" start through activating small, tight networks. Jesus himself said that the Kingdom of heaven is like a mustard seed. Amazing things happen when ordinary leaders live as listening disciples.

I know that John has shared this kind of teaching with some of the most powerful and influential leaders in the world. But what I really like is that this kind of "octane" is available to ordinary disciples. This is not just a book for pastors; this is a book for *you and me*. If you will begin to catch the rhythm of listening to the God of the Bible by following John's lead, you will become a better disciple and a better leader."

Alan Hirsch
Author | Activist | Dreamer
The Permanent Revolution, Untamed, The Forgotten Ways, The Shaping of Things to Come

Here's the thing: Without a proper rhythm of life, it is impossible to hear the voice of God and experience the leading of the Holy Spirit. Going "OUT" to the world or "IN" to your close relationships without the "UP" of daily listening to God lapses into empty activism or self-indulgence. Until we learn to abide and await direction from the Word of God in Scripture, we are, in Paul's words, little more than *"noisy gongs or clanging cymbals"* (1 Corinthians 13:1).

In saying this, I could not be more pleased that my friend John Chandler has written this *"**Praying**"* series through the Old Testament. Understand from the outset, this isn't an attempt to cover every chapter of the Old Testament. He is not trying to offer the final, definitive picture of what God says there. Far from it. He is instead inviting you to *join him* in his practice of listening to God, participating in the "UPward" relationship of abiding, resting, pausing, waiting, and listening – which usually precedes a word from God. **If you learn to do that in these selected chapters, you will learn to do so in many other chapters not covered here.**

Take the example of learning to ride a bicycle. Maybe you were taught to ride by a parent, sibling or friend who walked beside you as you started unsteadily. Walking alongside you slowly at first, then guiding until you gained momentum and confidence, they then let you go. The steering became easier as you learned to pedal more rapidly. And once you learned to ride a bike, you never forgot. This is what John is trying to do in these reflections. He is modeling the way, walking alongside of you, helping you gain speed – and he will let you go in order to explore on your own the rest of the Bible in all of its riches.

At least in my understanding, this is one of the most biblical ways of teaching. Jesus drew his disciples around him so they could learn by watching. Paul repeatedly said to his churches, *"Imitate me as I imitate Christ"* (I Corinthians 11:1, Philippians 3:17, 2 Thessalonians 3:7, Hebrews 13:7, etc.). John himself has a track record of offering his life and leadership to other disciples so that they can learn to grow in the rhythms of Jesus. And in this book, he is offering a way of imitation to you. We never get to innovation by mere information; it takes imitation as well. And if you will learn to imitate John's practice of listening daily to the Bible and expecting God to guide you, you will grow as a disciple of Jesus.

Maybe we can use a quick example.

Many of us have probably had someone in our church community approach us with a measure of frustration and say, "Can you help me read this book? No matter how much I try, I can't seem to understand what I read in the Bible. It doesn't always make sense." What do most of us do? Well, we probably give them a book that was particularly helpful for us; maybe we ask some questions; but we probably also show them *how we engage with the scriptures!* That's what we are talking about here. There's information we give, but then we flesh it out with a real-life example. We realize that the purpose of imitation is that it will lead to innovation.

I am particularly excited for the visual material accompanying these reflections. Don't let the simple nature of the sketches fool you. Their power is found not only in how they capture the big idea of the reflection. The drawings are powerful because they enable you to understand and pass along that big idea to another person. Again, true discipleship is not merely listening "UP" to God or taking information "IN" to your own heart. Until we pass along the word of God out to others, we have not "closed the circuit." And these illustrations will help you lead "OUT" by giving you a concrete way of sharing what you have heard. *It makes it reproducible!*

In my own experience, having visual material (LifeShapes) is a way of helping people who learn by sight and by touch in a different way than conceptual learners. Art makes material available to a whole different group of people, and perhaps to a whole different sector of your heart. These sketches are catchy, memorable, and portable. They can be cross-cultural and cross-generational. The artist, Jessica Luttrull, has done us a favor. She has made her work repeatable. By offering art that we can sketch to others, she has created a vehicle for us to grow in being disciples and making disciples.

In short, I hope you will not only read the book, but learn to imitate the way that is modeled here: to listen expectantly, discern clearly, and lead biblically. John is an apostolic leader, and I am seeing evidences of "torches" he is lighting with young leaders ("Uptick") and other Virginia Baptists who are imitating him as he imitates Christ. They are growing and paying it forward by teaching others to be disciples of Jesus. We want to see these torches become "bonfires," missional centers not only in Virginia, but around the world. I pray that as this book helps you set your rhythm of life with Jesus, your life will become a torch that will become a part of this larger bonfire.

Mike Breen
Global Leader, 3D Ministries | Pawleys Island, South Carolina
Author, *Building a Discipling Culture, Covenant and Kingdom*

Preface: *How this book began*

I experienced the great blessing of growing up in a time and place where reading the Bible was intrinsically valued as the path to personal transformation. If you wanted to know and grow with the God of Jesus Christ, then the first and best way to do that was to study the Bible.

My grandfather would quietly mention that he read entirely through a different translation of the Bible every year. My blind grandmother would listen to recorded cassette tapes of scripture and often memorize entire chapters at a time. In my Sunday School at Friendly Avenue Baptist Church in Greensboro, North Carolina, we turned in weekly offering envelopes with checkmark answers to the personal question, "Bible Read Daily?" Once I became a teenage disciple of Jesus Christ, I learned to read at bed time my "Good News" version of the Bible, with its simple but interesting stick-figure illustrations.

Bible study which began as an adolescent conviction then developed into adult academic pursuit at the university and seminary, and later a vocational habit as a pastor and teacher. I have since experimented with creative ways to continue engaging with the Bible diligently, such as listening to spoken scripture while riding my motorcycle. Leviticus is never as interesting as when blared at eighty miles an hour!

Several years, ago, my friend Mike Breen challenged me about the discipline of "winning the first battle of the day" – that is, to engage in listening conversation with God through the Bible before turning to the inbox and my work for that day. I decided to do away with my first-thing-in-the morning habit of two newspapers and ESPN SportsCenter, and devote myself instead to serious, daily reflection on one chapter of Scripture every day. With strong coffee and my cat at my side, I began to consolidate lessons and sermons from a quarter-century's worth of previous teaching alongside of new study, and to record the key notes in the margins of a single preaching Bible. What I initially feared would be an hour or two I couldn't spare every day became the best practice I undertook, as I became a calmer, clearer, more effective leader. As my personal muscle for the practice developed, so did my ability to lead others to do likewise.

A relational network is a powerful thing, and through one such network, I met a very important leader, one whose daily decisions impact untold numbers of people. The short version of the story is that my wife, Mary, and I began to pray daily for him. And I began to email this leader two to four brief reflections from the Old Testament as I studied every day. I tried to hone in on leadership insights and how a chapter might give guidance for daily decisions such leaders face. Whenever God impressed something upon me through daily study, I captured it in a brief email, and sent it forward.

I found this idea of leadership guidance to be a fascinating lens through which to engage with the Bible. I also found that whatever guidance I sent to this leader was often useful to share with others. Often I would diagram on the back of a napkin a simple picture to capture the core daily insight. Over time, as I tried to lead, teach, and mentor, this became a habit. After a year's worth of doing so, Mary suggested that I compile these reflections into a book.

There are 929 chapters in the Old Testament and I focused selectively and not comprehensively on some of what God had to say about leadership within the 249 chapters between Joshua and Esther. Though the title is **Praying the Kings**, this is only a convenient summary, and a bit misleading. Often the best leaders in these chapters are not kings but women, foot soldiers, unofficial and ordinary people without post or public recognition – but leaders nonetheless. This work starts in the book of Joshua, when the great leader Moses is gone, and *"there was no king in Israel; all the people did what was right in their own eyes"* (Judges 21:25). We end in the book of Esther, where the king and other official leaders are idiots, and the truest leaders are women without power or title. Between the books of Joshua and Esther are many demonstrations of what makes for good and bad leadership. What I share here only scratches the surface. I believe that anyone who will engage in disciplined listening to the material between Joshua and Esther will find many more (and better) insights about leadership than are captured here!

While I want these specific devotions to guide leaders in daily decisions, I hope even more deeply that they model the way to form habits or "build the muscles" of disciples to listen every day to God through scripture. When leaders are habitually disciplined to engage with the Bible about their leadership, they will be amazed at the guidance that comes from God. It is *"new every morning"* (Lamentations 3:23). I am certainly finding this to be true, as the verse with which my grandfather charged me at ordination to ministry is unfolding in my life:

> *"The Lord God has given me the tongue of a teacher, that I may know how to sustain the weary with a word. Morning by morning he wakens – wakens my ear to listen as those who are taught." – Isaiah 50:4*

I pray this work will help to waken your ear as you lead.

John P. Chandler

Introduction: *Goals, Audience, Methods*

Goals

The premise for this book is a simple one: reading the Bible expectantly can change your life as a leader. If you will discipline yourself to come to Scripture every day with the conviction that God will offer concrete guidance for your life and leadership, you won't be disappointed. There will be "fresh bread" given to you as surely as God gave Israel manna in the desert. And, when you learn to capture these biblical insights in simple pictures and pass them "on the back of a napkin" to other leaders, you will unlock great power for yourself and for many.

My goal is to model the way for you to do this so that you can build the muscle to make it the time signature in your rhythm of life.

Mike Breen teaches brilliantly of the imagery of the work of finding wisdom. Citing Job 28, he says that our job is to "dig" or "excavate" the precious gold of wisdom under the surface. Sometimes wisdom simply comes to us through an <u>eruption</u> of the Holy Spirit, like lava from beneath the earth's surface spouting from a volcano. Other times, we gain wisdom the hard way – through <u>erosion</u>, where suffering strips away the topsoil of our life, revealing precious but hard-won metals underneath. But beyond eruption and erosion is a third way: the way of <u>excavation</u>. Here, we dig a shaft beneath the surface soil until we find the gold underneath.

Here's a picture:

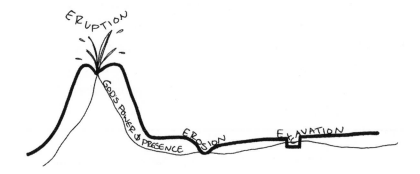

This book is not only a collection of nuggets I have mined and want to pass along, but is written in hopes that you will learn to be a miner, too. If you read and treat this simply as a collection of someone else's devotional thoughts and stop there, then I will have failed in what I hope to achieve. There's plenty more gold "down there." And my goal is to model the way until you learn to dig for yourself! (You know, teach a person to fish and ....) Again, I believe that if you excavate Scripture expectantly and with discipline, you will never be without the guidance of the Holy Spirit in very concrete ways that inform your life and leadership.

Audience

This book is for leaders. If you have formal or informal influence over another person, group, or situation, you are a leader. And you can benefit from turning to the Bible with an eye for what it has to say about leadership. I hope pastors and Bible teachers will be able to use this book, but even more, it is for managers, school teachers, bank tellers, students, CEOs and landscapers.

We look at the Old Testament period between Joshua and Esther because it is rife with examples of both the promise and failure of leaders. Moses and the patriarchs are gone and the great prophets are yet to come. People in official positions are often incompetent or wicked, teaching us that leadership never automatically proceeds from title. The entire period is a case study of the great good that can be done through effective leadership (even in dark times), as well as the costs of squandered leadership opportunities. In this sense, it is a treasure trove for leaders who want to learn on the dime of others and make good leadership calls today.

The great leaders from Joshua to Esther are great listeners to God. My conviction is that, for Christians, leadership should be viewed through the lens of discipleship. The best leaders of people are the best followers of Jesus. The core work of leading is to listen to our Leader before we try to lead anyone else anywhere else.

Dallas Willard has repeatedly stated that the two most important questions we can ask of Christians today are, "What's your plan for discipleship?" and "How's that plan working?" If leaders are disciples, and leaders are planners, then this book is an attempt to help you map out strategically a plan for listening that is at the heart of great leadership. In Willard's teaching, you will have to "abstain" from some things in order to detach from their claims on your ear, mind, eye, and heart. Such *abstinence* then leads to time and space for disciplines of *engagement*, where we are free to truly hear and prepared to respond to God. God has a word worth hearing, and if you will learn to listen daily, it will help you with self-leadership and with leading others. This is how to optimize our opportunities and indeed our lives!

Methods

There are several ways to picture how we want to build this muscle for listening to God, leading others, and optimizing our lives. Here's one:

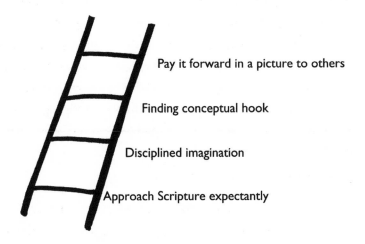

Pay it forward in a picture to others

Finding conceptual hook

Disciplined imagination

Approach Scripture expectantly

Here, we plan to come to the Bible every day out of confidence that it will be the most useful thing we can do as we prepare to lead. We come as part of the very rhythm of our life, like breakfast for our soul. Then, as we read with an eye for what God might say about leadership, we listen for a hook, a simple and straightforward word from God that emanates out of the characters, storyline, or direct teaching of the Scripture. Finally, as my friends in recovery say, "you can't keep it until you give it away." In other words, the leadership insights that come from the hook must be paid forward and passed along to someone else before they are fully activated in our own lives. Sharing what you have heard with someone else is the "activation code" or catalyst that brings the insight to life in leadership. Mastery comes through gifting to others.

I believe that the best way to do this is through a simple picture. Edward Tufte and Dan Roam have taught us that perhaps the best way to bring conceptual information to life and application is through simple, visual means. If you can't write it on the "back of a napkin," you haven't really absorbed the insight to the point where it is useful to you and others. Mike Breen, in using "LifeShapes," has understood this, and I have seen firsthand many times the power of a simple visual diagram to communicate vast leadership insights. Simple, visual information has the ability to be cross-cultural and multi-generational. It has the wherewithal to cut through the muck of words and get to the heart of action-oriented, mind-changing, behavior-modifying leadership.

Breen's triangle (of course) illustrates this:

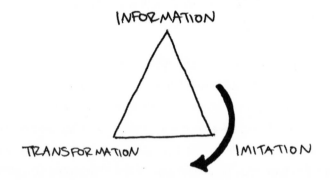

The great fallacy of how we grow is that we move straight from *Information* to *Transformation*. But "more informed" clearly does not automatically equate to "fully transformed." To get to *transformation*, one must first go through a process of *imitation*. We need models, mentors, demonstrations, living examples. We need people who can, step-by-step, show us how a word from God became part of our life, and how it can become a part of your life. This is why Paul repeatedly said to his young churches, *"Imitate me, just as I also imitate Christ"* (1 Corinthians 11:1). The Incarnation demonstrates that we need knowledge embodied, modeled, and lived out before it can become part of our way of being and doing. Only then does knowledge become wisdom and revelation:

Leadership (gained as we pay it forward by sketching it for another)

Wisdom/Revelation (gained as we capture the "hook," i.e. in a drawing)

Knowledge/Insight (gained as we engage with Scripture)

So, while God will impress upon us great insights while we engage with Scripture, those insights do not become a part of our transformation until we capture and then pass them along. And we can pass them along by sketching them out for another person to receive in such a way that they, too, can pay it forward.

Again, there are 929 chapters in the Old Testament and 249 in the books from Joshua to Esther. Here I have selected only ninety-nine, and by no means have come close to exhausting the insights available in any of those selected chapters. My aim is for this to be a how-to manual, not a coffee table book. Watch what I do here, and then imitate this habit in your own way. My hope is that you will learn to engage with Old Testament leaders in a way that informs the decisions you have to make every day as you lead people. My prayer is that, after practicing through this book, you will have built the muscles to do the work of mining on your own as you continue to excavate the Bible. I can promise that it will change you as a disciple and as a leader.

Operating Instructions: *How to use*

Before opening the Bible ...

Just do it. Begin the discipline of studying a chapter of the Bible a day on the very day you get this book. Don't procrastinate and don't try to wait until the beginning of a new book of the Bible or first day of the month or year.

Kneel. I suggest a beginning with a brief physical gesture, or ritual that will help you to put yourself in a posture of receiving. I use a kneeler bench outside of my bedroom door, so that before I walk out for the day, I have submitted to God for guidance. However you choose, ask God to open your heart to hearing as you submit yourself to the discipline of listening to the Bible.

Prepare your workspace. I find it very useful to have a certain desk where I do this work every day; it is part of a routine which helps form habit. It is a signal to my body and mind of what I am about to undertake. Bring with you a Bible you can write in, a pen, and a ruler. A notepad is useful for putting persistent distractions in a parking lot until later.

Plan. For me, writing key notes in a single Bible is useful. Working on a single chapter per day (or sometimes a slightly longer thought-unit) sets a consistent scope. Block off your daily calendar and notify those who need to know that you are unavailable during this time.

Praying the Kings

Win the first battle of the day. "Time" and "Space" are the media of creation in Genesis 1 and continue to be today. There will be a battle for your heart and for your attention. For me, I had to postpone reading two daily newspapers and discard *SportsCenter*. It will be vital to read the Bible before texts, email, Facebook, Twitter, etc. Turn the sound notifications off on all devices and resolve to open yourself to Scripture before engaging electronically.

While the Bible is open before you ...

Start with the Bible alone. Before looking at commentaries, annotations, or anything anyone else has said about the Scripture before you, give your chapter a chance to speak to you on its own terms. Read, re-read, and perhaps read aloud until you digest the chapter. I also practice by reading it in Spanish; if you know another language, use it to slow you down and think more richly about nuances.

Underline intuitively. When (re)reading the chapter of the day, highlight and underline intuitively. Where do words, phrases, sentences, verses, or even whole sections of Scripture jump off of the page at you? Don't over-think, but make notes of strong impressions.

Study alongside of church history. You can't know what the Bible means to me until you know what it meant to the people to whom it was written, and you can't know what the Bible meant until you actually listen to what it says. Beyond "impressionism" lays the rigorous examination of three thousand years of reflection by others who have engaged with the Bible. Pick a few trusted commentaries – and if you know don't whom to trust, ask someone who does – and let them serve as guides to help you listen to the Scripture. You don't want to do this *before* listening on your own to Scripture ... but you don't want to be the only one listening to the Scripture. For me, heroes like Walter Brueggemann are trustworthy guides to hearing the Bible on its own terms. Read what one or two commentaries say about your chapter. Take notes where the insights of others illumine your reading so that if you were to go back later to a page of Scripture, ideas for the interpretation of that passage would be on the page and ready to share.

Hone in. Now, after having used the wide-angle lens, narrow it back down. From your own impressions and from the insights gained by wider study, hone in on one focal verse. (At times, it may be a single word, the action of a character, or a short passage. Don't get too legalistic about it.) By this point, your underlining and notes will be great clues.

Receive again. As you hone in on your verse, ask God to reveal what he is trying to say about how you lead and how you might help others lead. This is what I mean by reading the Bible through the lens of leadership, and leadership through the lens of discipleship. Ask for a "word" from God. Using the key verse, ask the Lord to fix in your mind and heart for the day some divine direction or guidance. It may be as simple as a single word that you want to repeat throughout the day. Or, it could be a phrase, the verse itself, or illustration of a key story of the biblical text. Ask God for grace to remember and return to that word throughout that day. This is not hocus-pocus but more akin to Paul Ricoeur's "second naiveté."

After you have closed the Bible ...

Use "fresh bread." Before leaving the time and space of the "first battle of the day," commit to sharing in some venue (verbal or written) your received "word" from God (a verse/principle/story) during same day that you received it. Resolve to share what you have heard and learned with someone in a situation that will become apparent to you only once you are in it. Don't cram or force it, but go into the day open to sharing what you yourself have heard from Scripture and how it is affecting you. As often as not, you will be giving testimony as to how God is changing you as a leader as you will be offering input to someone else about how they lead.

Draw it on the back of a napkin. We close the loop when we pay forward to someone else what God has offered to us. Do so by sharing the word you have received with a very simple illustration or diagram. Such a picture gives you ways to "operationalize" insights into active leadership practice and make it useful in daily life. It will not only potentially help a person you are trying to lead; it will also finish the circuit for your own absorption of the word from God in your life.

JOSHUA 1

WHEN A BOOK IS A BETTER LEADER

"Joshua son of Nun was full of the spirit of wisdom, because Moses had laid his hands upon him ... Never since has there arisen a prophet in Israel like Moses, whom the Lord knew face to face." – Deuteronomy 34:9-10

"My servant Moses is dead. Now proceed to cross the Jordan, you and all this people, into the land that I am giving to them, to the Israelites." – Joshua 1:2

The "closing of the Torah" coincides with the death of Moses. And while this leader did well to pass along what he had been given to the next leader, Moses does not enter the Promised Land. Moses is dead, but God is not. The human leader is gone, but God's call and promise remain.

The people go in with not a Leader, but with a Book. They have, in the Torah, what they need to live faithfully. It does not depend on the charisma of a uniquely gifted prophet; the good life depends on faithfulness to what has been revealed to all the people through the words of God in Scripture.

Prayer: *God, grant us confidence in your revealed word of Scripture. Help us to lean wholly on what you have shown us there. Help us to remember that leaders come and go from the scene, but your revealed word stands forever as wisdom, truth, and guidance. In Jesus' name, Amen.*

JOSHUA 2

"Now then, since I have dealt kindly with you, swear to me by the Lord that you in turn will deal kindly with my family. Give me a sign of good faith ..." – Joshua 2:12

Joshua 2:9-13 is the longest consecutive speech by any woman in the Bible. Its speaker, Rahab, was Canaanite prostitute who aided Joshua and the Israelites in the overthrow of the very kind of government that consigned women and slaves to destitute, faceless existences. The center of her speech speaks of leadership as fundamentally an act of "kindness": *"Since I have dealt kindly with you, swear to me by the Lord that you in turn will deal kindly with my family"* (v. 12).

As an act of leadership, kindness is:

- ≈ Sticking your neck out;

- ≈ Providing shelter as an act of righteousness;

- ≈ Putting your business on the line for something godly;

- ≈ Encouraging people so that God can move miraculously.

It is no wonder that in the genealogy of Matthew 1, Rahab is one of four women mentioned as a forbear of the ultimate expression of God's kindness, Jesus Christ. Louder is not profounder, tougher is not superior, and meaner doesn't mean you are a better leader. Sometimes we lead in courageous, righteous, godly, and encouraging modes. Sometimes the best leadership is an exercise in kindness.

JOSHUA 3

BAPTISM INTO LEADERSHIP

"When the soles of the feet of the priests who bear the ark of the Lord, the Lord of all the earth, rest in the waters of the Jordan, the waters of the Jordan flowing from above shall be cut off; they shall stand in a single heap." – Joshua 3:13

consecrate
yourself

Recalling the crossing of the Israelites out of Egypt through the Red Sea, and looking ahead to the time Jesus would himself cross the Jordan, this story undergirds the symbolism of baptism, our immersion in the person of Jesus (Romans 6:4). Just as Abraham was directed first to *"go"* before God would *"show"* him, here the people of God are called first to place their feet in the river before the river parts. It is an exercise in behaving your way into believing! Once they do this, the people begin to complete the Exodus deliverance and wilderness wanderings. They enter for the first time the promised land, where their assignment is to form a new tribe of justice to overthrow corruption and unholiness.

The geography of their journey is symbolically significant. On a merely topographical level, it reflects the landscape of the Jordan valley, through which people descend on three levels:

1. The Ghor, a fertile upper level, fit for cultivation;

2. The middle level, a desolate desert full of clay;

3. The Zor, an ancient jungle inhabited by wild beasts.

But the description of the path which God's people must walk is more than mere topography. To cross the Jordan symbolizes this journey down, and then back up and out – a fitting symbol for the life promised in our baptism. The people are called to descend, immerse, and be raised. And leadership, then and now, means willingly going down-in-up personally, and also inviting and leading others with you through this same journey.

John P. Chandler 25

JOSHUA 5

WORKING THE CROPS

"On the day after the Passover, on that very day, they ate the produce of the land, unleavened cakes and parched grain. The manna ceased on the day they ate the produce of the land, and the Israelites no longer had manna; they ate the crops of the land of Canaan that year." **– Joshua 5:11-12**

Praying the Kings

Like the circumcision ritual mentioned just before it (Joshua 5:2-9), the Passover is a rite of passage to adulthood. Eugene Peterson has suggested that the first five books of the Bible reflect five life stages: Genesis (conception), Exodus (birth and toddlerhood), Leviticus (childhood, with lots of rules), Numbers (teenage rebellion), Deuteronomy (entering adulthood).

After birth in the Exodus and teenage rebellion in the wilderness, here in Joshua, the people are in the process of becoming adults and entering the Promised Land. No longer will the people of God, like baby birds, be fed straight from the hand of God. Now they will inherit good land, but they will have to take personal and corporate adult responsibility to work the crops. This was a daunting responsibility, but also a call to justice: to overthrow a society of haves/have-nots through taking ownership of life in the good land promised by God.

Leaders are grown-ups. They don't expect to be fed but to feed. They know that they must work the crops in order to see the harvest.

Prayer: *O Lord, let me today take grown-up responsibility for my life and leadership. In the name of the One, Jesus Christ, who was born a child that we might grow up, Amen.*

Your servant!

JOSHUA 7

TAKING
DEVOTED
THINGS

"The Lord said to Joshua, "Stand up! Why have you fallen on your face? Israel has sinned; they have transgressed my covenant that I have imposed on them. They have taken some of the devoted things; they have stolen, they have acted deceitfully, and they have put them among their own belongings. Therefore the Israelites are unable to stand before their enemies ..." – Joshua 7:10-12

The winning streak of victories since entering the Promised Land is over, as the Israelites are routed at Ai (which means "ruin"). Why are they ruined? Not because of the might of external enemies, but because of covetousness, lying, and stealing – rot from the inside of the tribe. Echoing Eve and foreshadowing early church leaders Ananias and Sapphira (Acts 5), a man in Israel named Achan stole booty from a defeated enemy and hid it for himself, defying instruction to destroy it completely. Achan didn't need the goods for sustenance; he was rich. But like many bad kings to come, this wealthy but envious man put the whole community at risk through his greed. God describes the sin of Achan as *an outrageous thing in Israel* (v. 15).

To his credit, the spiritual leader Joshua responds decisively. He laments the sin (vv. 6ff), searches for the root cause (vv. 16-18), elicits a confession (vv. 19-21), and enacts clear-eyed and swift justice without hesitation (vv. 22-26), killing Achan.

Often people look to external forces to blame for their defeats and troubles. But this is a story that teaches us that leaders must have an eye in the mirror as well as an eye on the horizon. Leaders teach communities to look in their own midst. They do not tolerate hoarding, deceit, and acts of personal selfishness; they know that such things endanger not only the perpetrator but also the whole community. And no leader is willing to let the sins of one pollute the cause of many.

JOSHUA 10

"On the day when the Lord gave the Amorites over the Israelites, Joshua spoke to the Lord; and he said in the sight of Israel, "Sun, stand still at Gibeon, and Moon, in the valley of Aijalon." And the sun stood still, and the moon stopped, until the nation took vengeance on their enemies."
– Joshua 10:12-13

After the sin of Achan and the unearthing of internal rot in chapter 7, the enemies of Israel become more confident and aggressive. A hostile coalition, who did not appreciate the threat to their unchallenged and tyrannical rule, arose against Joshua and his forces.

The battles are bloody, unsparing, and even offensive to modern sensibilities. Why? They are captured as an unblinking part of scripture because they represent not only historical skirmishes, but are also deeply symbolic, even mythic. Repeatedly, chapter 10 lists instances of the Lord fighting and intervening on behalf of his people. Most pointedly, God answers Joshua's prayer and causes the sun to stand still: *"The sun stopped in midheaven, and did not hurry to set for about a whole day. There has been no day like it before or since, when the Lord heeded a human voice; for the Lord fought for Israel"* (vv. 13f).

This is far more than an example of asking God to bless a victory we want. This is an example of God's war over the powers of chaos that began in Genesis 1, when God separated the dry land from the waters. This war will end in Revelation 19-22, where God will bring about a perfectly ordered holy city from heaven to earth. From beginning to end, the Bible describes God's war versus the powers of chaos which oppress and confuse the world. And when, like Joshua, we join in that truly holy battle, we can ask for and receive help greater than any power in the natural and human worlds.

JOSHUA 14

TAPPING THE TRAITS OF COMPANION LEADERS

"Here I am today, eighty-five years old. I am still as strong today as I was on the day that Moses sent me; my strength now is as my strength was then, for war, and for going and coming. So now give me this hill country of which the Lord spoke on that day ..." – Joshua 14:10-12

Caleb, along with Joshua, was one who "wholeheartedly followed the Lord" (v. 14). Because they were great followers of God, they were great leaders of people. The outcome was that for long stretches of Caleb's influence, "the land had rest from war" (v. 15).

Scholars note that while Joshua was strongly linked with his predecessor Moses, Caleb is more connected with the much-later king David through an emphasis in both on faithful obedience to God. Because of his youthful start and long-term leadership, Caleb would serve as a model for later faithful, young kings like Josiah (2 Kings 22).

Whereas Joshua was often a fiery, outspoken, blunt, and decisive leader, Caleb's strengths tended toward steadiness, cool, and long-term clarity. In terms of the Galatians 5:22 list of the fruit of the spirit, he typically embodied "patience" (ability to stay in hard moments), "faithfulness" (perseverance to do so over the long haul), and "self-control" (ability to temper and delay immediate reactions for long-term gain).

Three short notes about Caleb's life that can serve as exemplary leadership:

He did so for "forty-five years" ... and at "eighty-five years old" was still seeking leadership challenges: "So now give me this hill country of which the Lord spoke ...."

His leadership evolved over the course of his life. Whereas in younger years his energies were devoted "for war, and for going and coming," near the sunset of his life, he wanted best to deploy a still-ample supply of his "strength" for purposes more suited to his age and life stage.

Caleb exhibited traits of leadership complementary and not identical to those of his companion leader, Joshua.

Blessed is the leader today who brings alongside a very different companion leader whose complementary strengths benefit many for long-term impact!

Exercise: *Can you identify a potential companion leader to come alongside of you whose leadership would complement what God is calling you to do? Ask God to give you the eyes to recognize such a person. And if you already know who this person is, then "make the ask!"*

John P. Chandler   33

JOSHUA 17

CLEARING THE FOREST

" ... but the hill country shall be yours, for though it is a forest, you shall clear it and possess it to its farthest borders; for you shall drive out the Canaanites, though they have chariots of iron, and though they are strong." – Joshua 17:18

In the Bible, geography is often a clue to theology. A mountain is often a place of revelation – Moses on Sinai, Jesus in the Sermon on the Mount. An ocean is often the locale for God's battle over the forces of chaos – Noah and the Flood, Jonah and the whale. And is no mistake that the Bible begins in a garden and ends in a city.

In Joshua 17, there is a clear evolution of geography in the command of God to his people about the land. The divine command is to transform space from:

Forest → City
Thicket → Garden
Wilderness → Inheritance

As they move into *"hill country,"* they are to make this *"forest"* inhabitable by <u>clearing</u> and <u>possessing</u> it, and <u>driving out</u> strong enemies with advanced weapons. (No one said it would be easy!)

The command for the people to *"clear it"* is interesting because it is the only time the verb is used of humans in the Old Testament. Typically, the work of ordering creation from chaos is spoken of as the work of God. But here, Joshua speaks of the transformation of thicket into park as the work of God's people to *"clear"* as part of God's greater project.

Biblical forests are abodes of wild beasts (Psalm 80:13). Leaders are called to join God in the work of clearing the forests so that they become gardens of human inhabitation and beauty.

JOSHUA 20-22

CITIES THAT EMBODY SANCTUARY

"The Lord commanded through Moses that we be given towns to live in ..." – **Joshua 21:2**

Israel has bequeathed to us several core disciplines that remind us of God's ownership and our stewardship of all things. The "first fruits" or "tithe" gift we owe reminds us that, in all things, God owns and we rent. The Sabbath is our weekly cue that our days and our work belong to the Lord. And here, Joshua names cities of refuge and sanctuary as a description of ideal and advanced community in harmony with divine intentions.

These cities function in several ways:

- To give sanctuary and asylum in such a way that breaks cycles of revenge and retribution (Joshua 20). They are places where justice is to rule over mob spirit.

- To be "Torah centers" for holy living. The operating instructions for life in these towns:

  - *"observe/keep the commandments"*

  - *"love the Lord your God"*

  - *"walk in his ways"*

  - *"hold fast to him"*

  - *"serve him with all your heart and with all your soul" (22:5).*

- To distribute leadership locally – communities will not be ruled by a central king, but by *"heads of the families of the tribes of the Israelites"* (21:1). This foreshadows the *"holy priesthood"* and *"spiritual house"* (1 Peter 2:5) where all of God's people share in the creation of the beloved community.

Yet again, biblical leadership is fundamentally about creating high-functioning community. We are to build cities that embody sanctuary, both in the sense of refuge for the stranger, and holiness for those who inhabit the towns.

John P. Chandler

JOSHUA 23

"Therefore be very steadfast to observe and do all that is written in the book of the law of Moses, turning aside from it neither to the left or to the right, so that you may not be mixed with these nations left here among you, or make mention of the names of their gods, or swear by them, or serve them, or bow yourselves down to them, but hold fast to the Lord your God, as you have done to this day."
– Joshua 23:6-8

Joshua's farewell address, like Moses' at the end of Deuteronomy, is largely a warning against complacency. People can get slack after they have won their battles, achieved their goals, arrived at their destination. And, because the people of God are not to sequester from or eliminate nations that do not follow the Lord, there will always be opportunity to compromise and syncretize.

Joshua 23 describes three fundamental spheres of temptation:

> ☞ **Lips** – *"do not make mention of the names of their gods or swear by them,"*

> ☞ **Hands** – *"do not serve them … but hold fast to the Lord your God,"* and

> ☞ **Knees** – *"do not … bow yourselves down to them."*

Later leaders would faithlessly violate in each of these spheres of temptation. They would take rash oaths with their lips (Hosea 4:15), seize with their hands by blatant violence (1 Kings 21), and brazenly bow the knee in worship to local deities (1 Kings 16:31).

Leaders today would do well to take an audit of their lips, hands, and knees as critical spheres of temptation. Am I most tempted to say things I should not say? Take hold of things I should not grasp? Walk to a place or kneel to an interest not fitting?

And perhaps these audits are most fitting not during times of duress, but in days of success and plenty.

Exercise: *Circle lips, hand, or knee as today's challenge. Ask for God to bring this warning to your remembrance today, and pray for grace to withstand temptation in this sphere of your life and leadership today.*

JOSHUA 24

PUTTING AWAY
ANCESTOR AND
IMPERIAL GODS

*"Now therefore revere the Lord, and serve him in sincerity
and in faithfulness; put away the gods that your ancestors
served beyond the River and in Egypt, and serve the Lord. ...
as for me and my household, we will serve the Lord."*
– Joshua 24:14-15

Joshua's final act of leadership is to call for decision from leaders, and to place himself in the middle of that responsibility by casting his own ballot. The capstone of his leadership is to challenge obedience to the pinnacle of the Ten Commandments: *"You shall have no other gods before me"* (Exodus 20:3).

Just who are these other gods that vie for the attention and allegiance of the people? Joshua highlights two categories of gods unworthy of our total devotion:

1. *"gods your ancestors served beyond the River"* – these are fetish gods, local deities, traditional or ancestor-based reverences. The core biblical response is that such gods are fundamentally projections of human beings, mere extrapolations of wishful thinking. Worshiping them would be, essentially, elevating something in the created realm beyond its station.

2. *"gods served ... in Egypt"* – these are national, imperial, colonial, or military gods. They are spiritual attempts at legitimating national ambitions. Such gods are merely tools of the state, subordinate and in service to power and throne. These gods merely do what kings want them to do.

Freud rightly critiqued <u>ancestor</u> gods as human projection, and Marx rightly judged <u>imperial</u> gods as opiate of the masses. (Ironically, Joshua and Moses beat both of them to the punch.)

Sadly, the book of Joshua ends with a worthy example that is subsequently not followed. From the books of Judges through the end of the prophets, Israel's sad legacy is that of leaders and people who serve the wrong gods, ancestor and imperial gods. The story is a cautionary tale and a challenge for every leader today: which God/god will I choose to serve?

John P. Chandler   41

JUDGES 1

RIGHTEOUSNESS TOWARD WOMEN

"After the death of Joshua, the Israelites inquired of the Lord,
"Who shall go up first for us against the Canaanites, to fight
against them?" – Judges 1:1

The book of Judges is a story of degeneration between leaders. Joshua is dead and David is yet to come. So in between, we have flawed judges – like Samson – who show some strengths but are marred with lethal weaknesses.

One of the ways we can see the crumbling of Israelite society is in the state of marriage and treatment of women. In the first chapter of Judges, Caleb's daughter-in-law Achsah is happily riding a donkey to meet her hero husband and be blessed with a gift. By mid-book, the time of Samson, relations with Delilah are marked by seduction and betrayal (16:18). By the end of the book of Judges, the Levite's concubine (unnamed!) has been gang-raped, dismembered, and sent on a donkey in pieces throughout the land.

One of the ways Israel was sent into the land to overthrow oppression and model justice was to model a more loving and righteous treatment of women and marriage.

Prayer: *Dear Lord, thank you for the gift of Eve, who is to be loved, honored, and cherished as we together work the garden in which you have placed us. Grant us a vision of society in which she might flourish, and all of us flourish because she does. In the name of the one who walked in this way with women, Jesus Christ, Amen.*

JUDGES 3

TAKING THE SWORD
TO FAT CATS

*"(Ehud) said, "I have a message from God for you." So he
rose from his seat. Then Ehud reached with his left hand,
took the sword from his right thigh, and thrust it into Eglon's
belly; the hilt also went in after the blade, and the fat closed
over the blade, for he did not draw the sword out of his belly;
and the dirt came out." – Judges 3:20-22*

Praying the Kings

In the story of Judge Ehud (one of 12 sent by God to deliver Israel from oppression gained by her own folly) and King Eglon (a foreign king empowered by God to administer deserved punishment), two enlightening details stand out:

> ❧ Judge Ehud was *"left-handed"* (v. 15)

> ❧ King Eglon was *"a very fat man"* (v. 17)

Ehud's left-handedness was a symbol of his surprising ambidexterity, which gave him (and later Israel, see Judges 20:16) an amazing competitive advantage in warfare. Though smaller, Ehud was successfully empowered to overthrow oppression and destroy the king.

Eglon was a "fat cat." This is not a judgment on his obesity but a statement on his amazing strength and resources." As such, he symbolized those who had gained much at the expense of others.

Interestingly, Eglon was brought down by Ehud's *"sword."* In the same way, we look forward to the return of the Lord Jesus, who will one day come with a *"sharp, two-edged sword"* in his mouth to deliver (Revelation 1:16). Until that day, the word of Jesus still comes to those who would work toward his justice as a *"living and active two-edged sword"* (Hebrews 4:12).

John P. Chandler 45

JUDGES 4-5

the Leader

"Then Deborah and Barak son of Abinoam sang on that day, saying: "When locks are long in Israel, when people offer themselves willingly – bless the Lord!" – Judges 5:1

Barak is remembered later in the Bible (1 Samuel 12:11, Hebrews 11:32) for leading Israel to a great spiritual and military victory. Here are a few marks of his wise leadership:

> ꙼ His primary work was to partner with Deborah, an oracle and wise judge who was the true point-leader in the victory of Israel over the oppression of the Canaanites. He came when she summoned (4:6) and obeyed her word from God.

> ꙼ He allowed himself to be strengthened and encouraged when fluttering (vv. 4:8f) by the fearlessness of his partner.

> ꙼ He made as a spiritual matter (v. 6) the technological ("*chariots*" of v. 7), economic (blocked trade routes of 5:6f), and sexual (5:30) exploitation of the weak by the powerful.

> ꙼ He was able to allow those not in visible command (Jael in 4:17ff) do the key work and strike the decisive blows that led to victory. He got the credit historically, but without the women doing the leading, there would have been no victory.

May God remember Barak not for his great individual leadership but for his willingness to partner with many in the victory over those who would oppress!

John P. Chandler 47

JUDGES 7

JARS,
TORCHES,
TRUMPETS,
SWORDS

"So the three companies blew the trumpets and broke the jars, holding in their left hands the torches, and in their right hands the trumpets to blow; and they cried, "A sword for the Lord and for Gideon!" – Judges 7:20

In this one verse lays the symbols of everything that was right – and was wrong – with Gideon, a leader who could never quite trust that God would work through him to get the job done. Note these three symbols:

> ⮞ *Jars* – representing the emptiness of oppressive systems against which the Lord is opposed (Jeremiah 19:11);

> ⮞ *Torches* – light to illuminate the coming of a new, enlightened society (Isaiah 60:1-3); and

> ⮞ *Trumpets* – heralds of the Jubilee overturning of injustice to restructure the world (Leviticus 25:9)

Yet within the same verse lie the seeds of the unfaith (7:2, 10), arrogance, and discord (8:1-3) that undermined the enterprise: Gideon chose to take credit for what belonged to God alone: "*a sword for the Lord and for Gideon.*"

Is it possible for an insecure leader who craves recognition to undo with one hand what s/he has done with the other?

Prayer: *O Lord of all, thank you for filling the human spirit with incredible capacity – so much more than we might dare to imagine. But thank you that you are infinitely, qualitatively, different and transcendent. Teach us the wisdom of when to summon what you have given us, and teach us when to depend on and give credit to you alone for what can only be done by your hand. In the name of Jesus who embodied this power and humility, Amen.*

JUDGES 8

"As soon as Gideon died, the Israelites relapsed ..."
– Judges 8:33

By the end of Gideon's story in Judges 8, we see the outcomes of a gifted but wavering and ultimately deeply flawed leader. He seems driven by disproportionate revenge (vv. 7, 16, 21). And while he nobly refuses to be made king (v. 23), he more subtly agrees to be an oracle for the people, repeating the Exodus 32 tragedy of fashioning a golden calf (vv.24-27).

The final measure of Gideon's leadership was found not in his days, in which there was "rest" in the land and death "*at a good old age*." The assessment at the end of the day was this:

> "*As soon as Gideon died, the Israelites relapsed and prostituted themselves with the Baals ... the Israelites did not remember the Lord their God, who had rescued them from the hand of all their enemies on every side; and they didn't not exhibit loyalty ... in return for all the good that he had done in Israel.*" **(Judges 8:34-35)**

What is the evaluation of a leader who accomplished some heroic measures during a lifetime, but whose successors immediately relapsed into the situations which merited heroic rescue in the first place? Granted, each person and generation bears fundamental responsibility for itself; as the prophet Ezekiel would later say, "*the soul that sins is the soul that dies.*" But leaders do have an opportunity to set future generations in a position to succeed – or fail.

Truly, the merits of our leadership will be judged based on the outcomes generations out.

JUDGES 9

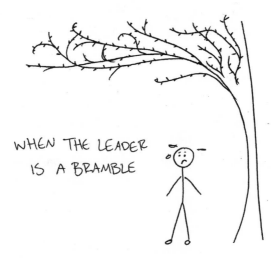

WHEN THE LEADER IS A BRAMBLE

"So all the trees said to the bramble, 'You come and reign over us.' And the bramble said to the trees, 'If in good faith you are anointing me king over you, then come and take refuge in my shade; but if not, let fire come out of the bramble and devour the cedars of Lebanon.'" – **Judges 9:15**

The story of Gideon concludes, sadly, with his son Abimilech and his nightmare reign (Judges 9). Abimilech's laundry list of offenses: he

> ∽ put clan over covenant (v. 2);

> ∽ installed himself as king through violence rather than God's call (v. 4);

> ∽ covered his misdeeds with a veneer of religiosity (v. 6); and

> ∽ was a "*bramble*" who gave neither shade nor rest to his people (vv. 15ff).

The only mention of God in the whole sorry mess is in verse 23, which said that "*God sent an evil spirit between Abimilech and his enemies.*" The final outcome was widespread death and a city sown with salt (v. 45), left in worse shape than Gideon first found it before his works of deliverance.

Abimilech's death at the hands of a woman is not on the insult on his legacy, but a final warning that those who elevate tribe over God ultimately find their ruin and cause the ruin of many.

Prayer: *Lord, we believe that you place these horrifying stories of terrible leaders in the Bible to warn us into remembering that you are our true King, our one and only leader. Help us to learn from the tragic decisions of others, and to build on rather than destroy the good legacies we have inherited. We reject leadership by violence and look forward to the day of your peaceable Kingdom, best made known to us in Jesus Christ, in whom we pray, Amen.*

John P. Chandler   53

JUDGES 11

"For I have opened my mouth to the Lord, and I cannot take back my vow." – Judges 13:35

The story of judge Jephthah and his only daughter is a tragic tale of unbelief and the costs of manipulation through words. Both *"son of a prostitute"* and *"mighty warrior"* (v. 1), Jephthah is a man without an inheritance (v. 2) and who is elevated as a national leader because he could talk, and he could fight (vv. 9-11). When a nation defines its chief problems as military, this is the sort of leader it gets.

Part of fighting was talking, and part of talking was making vows. Throughout his life, Jephthah gets what he wants through negotiating. When talks break down, he turns to force. This pattern of "argue → vow → kill" marks his leadership. Asking God for a military victory, he rashly promises a *"burnt offering"* (v. 31) of the first thing that comes through his door. Only, the thing turns out to be his *"only child"* (v. 35). And the rest of the sad (and very disturbing) story is that Jephthah holds his vow in higher esteem than his daughter, and he sacrifices her. More than any national victory, this is how we remember this judge – as a man who valued his vow more than his child.

Like Gideon putting out a fleece (Judges 6:36-40), Jephthah's is a story of unbelief, impatience, and an attempt to manipulate a situation (and God) with words. We can only shudder to think of how many children have been sacrificed through the ages because of the rash vows people in charge have made.

Jesus spoke of a higher righteousness than leading by verbal manipulation. Rather than taking sides as to the types of vows one should make, he instead spoke of leading through character: *"Let your word be 'Yes, Yes' or 'No, No'; anything more than this comes from the evil one"* (Matthew 5:37). Leaders today who follow Jesus will lead not through manipulative and rash words. We believe it is better leadership – and certainly better for the children who will not be sacrificed.

John P. Chandler   55

JUDGES 13-16

NAGGED, PESTERED,
TIRED, AND TOLD

"Finally, after she had nagged him with her words day after day, and pestered him, he was tired to death. So he told her his whole secret ..." – **Judges 16:16-17**

Praying the Kings

Samson is the epitome of the judges of Israel – a comic/tragic mixture of profound abilities and fatal flaws. He has both unparalleled strength, and the ability to be brought down by giving in to a terrible temper and a weakness for women. Ultimately, his is a story of unfulfilled promise: *"But he did not know that the Lord had left him"* (16:20). He killed many of Israel's enemies but destroyed himself in the process.

More than a historical figure, Samson is a cautionary parable of Israel itself. The chosen people have remarkable and God-given strength, yet are simultaneously subject to temptation that can enfeeble them. Just as Samson has a secret (his strength is in his hair, the sign of his covenant with God), so too do the people of God: their strength is in their covenant with the Lord. With Samson, with Israel, if you give up the secret, your strength goes away and you are destroyed.

Instructively, the secret is not seized from them by force but given away willingly and by compromise. Temptress Delilah (Arabic for "flirt") seduced Samson by relentless pinpricks to give away his secret, his identity. She *"nagged,"* and *"pestered"* him until *"he was tired to death."* Nibbled to death by ducks, he gave in, told his secret, and lost his soul and strength. He was captured, bound, blinded, and put in a mill for the sport of his captors. Sin binds, sin blinds, sin grinds.

Studies show that someone who has an affair first completes at least sixteen prior mental scenarios or actual conversations envisioning and moving toward the fulfillment of those possibilities. Most leaders don't sell out in one fell swoop but in a thousand tiny compromises. We are nagged and pestered by small sell-outs, and being tired may be one of our chief dangers.

The final outcomes of our leadership may be measured in the small decisions of faithfulness we are required to make every day.

John P. Chandler

JUDGES 21

MISTREATING WOMEN

"In those days there was no king in Israel; all the people did what was right in their own eyes." – Judges 21:25

Praying the Kings

The entire book of Judges is a story of the degeneration of Israel in the land of Canaan as it abandoned Yahweh as its king and whored after the gods of other nations (and their corresponding oppressive social practices). One of the great symbols of this degeneration is seen in the climactic and horrifying story of Judges 19-21, the gang-rape and dismemberment of the Levite's concubine.

This unnamed woman is further abused after her death by being made a propaganda symbol by which Israelites destroy tens of thousands of their fellow citizens, with special violence against women. By the end of the book (chapter 21), women are kidnapped, trafficked, and forced into marriages. They are acted upon rather than being actors in God's peaceable kingdom.

The abuse of women is the final symbol of a society gone terribly wrong, where "*there was no king in Israel; all the people did what was right in their own eyes*" (v. 25).

But the last verse is never the last verse with God – the next book in the Bible is the book of **Ruth**. Stay tuned, God may be up to something on behalf of women after all!"

RUTH 1

RESPONDING TO FAMINE AND BARRENNESS

"Then she started to return with her daughters-in-law from the country of Moab, for she had heard in the country of Moab that the Lord had considered his people and given them food." – Ruth 1:6

In the book of Ruth, much of the story centers on the activities of human actors (Ruth, Naomi, and Boaz). Each person embodies – contrary to the lawless spirit of their time – a deep kindness, loyalty, and unselfishness. They represent the "peaceable kingdom" envisioned in the messianic hopes of Isaiah 9:1-2: *"But there will be no gloom for those who were in anguish"* ... and, *"The people who walked in darkness have seen a great light."*

In fact, throughout the book of Ruth, the Lord intervenes in only two instances:

1. In response to <u>famine</u>, *"the Lord had considered his people and given them food"* (1:6), and

2. In response to <u>barrenness</u>, *"when they came together, the Lord made her conceive, and she bore a son"* (4:13).

Perhaps the structure of the story is its major clue: when human actors have done everything in their power to live peaceably and with kindness, at the point when they can do no more, the Lord will intervene. God is never too late – but is seldom early!

A leader like Ruth will navigate many decisions: to remain faithfully with her mother-in-law, to journey away from her homeland to a strange place, to deal effectively with Boaz. But there is also a time to let God do what only God can do. No individual can deal finally with famine and barrenness. But God can. And wise is the leader who lets God do what only God can do.

RUTH 3-4

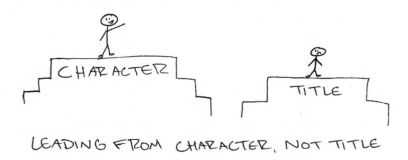

LEADING FROM CHARACTER, NOT TITLE

"And now, my daughter, do not be afraid, I will do for you all that you ask, for all the assembly of the people know that you are a worthy woman." – **Ruth 3:11**

The short story of Ruth is one of staggering reversals. In the span of four chapters, the people of God move from:

Famine → Food supplied
Xenophobia → Outsiders included
Barrenness → Heir produced
Widows and orphans → Community of provision
Sadness → Profound hope

None of these reversals come about because of the power of judges (like Samson) or wealth of kings (like Solomon). They happen because of the fundamental goodness and faithfulness of Ruth, combined with the discernment and generosity of Boaz.

These are honorable people, in an honorable relationship, who are known as honorable by all in their community. They don't hold particularly powerful positions in the community, but they hold something much more valuable: character. And because they live faithfully when few are looking, they are used by God in the transformation of something large and important.

It is no small thing that king David and eventually King Jesus descended from the line of Ruth and Boaz. That lineage is one of a thousand ways that the Bible emphasizes that character comes before competence, faithfulness comes before influence, and integrity comes before we have the platform to create change.

Like Mother Teresa, who dealt with world poverty by dealing with the single person in front of her in a Calcutta slum, a good leader begins leading long before they have a significant position, title, or platform of leadership.

1 SAMUEL 1

LENDING OUR CHILDREN

"For this child I prayed; and the Lord has granted me the petition that I made to him. Therefore I have lent him to the Lord; as long as he lives, he is given to the Lord." She left him there for the Lord." – 1 Samuel 1:27-28

Stories of long-barren women who bear offspring in unusual fashion or late in life have a special place in the Bible:

- Sarah cannot conceive until old age (Genesis 17:16-19);

- Rebekah struggled until giving birth to twins (Genesis 25:21-26);

- Rachel's infertility leads to great angst, rash action, family strife, and ultimately her death in childbirth (Genesis 30);

- The mothers of Samson (Judges 13:2-5) and John the Baptist (Luke 1:5-17) struggle spiritually, receive angelic visitations, and make vows about their sons once conceiving.

It is no wonder that the birth of Jesus to Mary is described with echoes of these stories. Only God can overcome barrenness, God hears the prayers of long-suffering women, and God uses unconventional family situations for great things.

Most of these features find their place in the story of Hannah. She was *"deeply distressed," "wept bitterly,"* and was full of *"great anxiety and vexation"* over her childlessness. She was upset to the point of people thinking she was *"drunk"* (vv. 10, 13-16). When she did conceive, her response was exemplary:

- She connected his conception and birth with God's response to her prayer, naming the boy Samuel because *"I have asked him of the Lord"* (v. 20);

- She modeled *"sacrifice"* for and with the child (v. 24); and

- Instead of clutching to the child, she consecrated him to God's purposes (v. 27).

Quite the opposite of a helicopter parent, Hannah models ideal leadership. She understands that her role is that of a steward, not an owner...that her time of influence is temporary, not permanent ...that the life of her precious son finally belongs to God's guidance rather than hers alone. If every leader could understand that whatever or whoever they lead is simply *"lent"* from the Lord, there would be cause for great rejoicing!

John P. Chandler   65

1 SAMUEL 3

CROSSING WHERE
IT'S NARROW

*"Now the Lord came and stood there, calling as before,
"Samuel! Samuel!" And Samuel said, "Speak, for your servant
is listening." – 1 Samuel 3:10*

There are many stories of dramatic conversions in the Bible. Most famously, Saul becomes Paul because of his visionary experience with Jesus on the Damascus Road (Acts 9). A dying thief turns toward Jesus on the cross (Luke 23:40-43). Even a Roman centurion participating in the execution of Christ turns to proclaim, "*Truly this man was God's Son!*" (Mark 15:39).

But the story of Samuel tells a different story of conversion. Here, a mother Hannah prays for her young boy before he is even conceived (1 Samuel 1:9). Samuel is consecrated to God for divine service as an infant (1:28). Raised in the temple under the tutelage of the priest Eli; "*the boy Samuel grew up in the presence of the Lord*" (2:21, 3:1).

So it was no surprise that Samuel was "*in the temple of the Lord, where the ark of God was*" (v. 3) when God called him by name. It takes a couple of hiccups before the boy Samuel, with some help from Eli, figures out that it is the Lord who is trying to speak to him. (Not every word from God to us is a high-noon, Damascus Road type of encounter!) Samuel opens his ears and heart to what God wants to say to and through him. He begins to grow in his development as a "*trustworthy prophet of the Lord*" (v. 20). He becomes a giant spiritual leader engaged in a life-long conversation with God.

Preacher John Claypool has said that Samuel "crossed the stream at a narrow place." His conversion was not a dramatic gulfing of the Mississippi, but a short hop over the water.

We leaders do well to understand that what is hard and dramatic for some people is more familiar and navigable for others. We can cultivate environments and experiences which acclimate people toward the direction we are trying to lead them. They have to make their own decisions about jumping over the water, but we can set them up to do so where their odds for making it to the other side increase. Wise is the leader who makes it possible for people to cross the stream where it is narrow.

John P. Chandler

1 SAMUEL 8

"Then all the elders of Israel gathering together and came to Samuel at Ramah, and said to him, "You are old and your sons do not follow in your ways; appoint for us, then, a king to govern us, like other nations." – 1 Samuel 8:4-5

There are two nations pivotal for understanding the Old Testament: Egypt and Babylon. The books of Samuel were written as part of an effort to explain how Israel spiraled down from the heights of Exodus from Egypt to the depths of the Exile in Babylon.

Much of the trouble began with a leadership or succession crisis. Samuel was a true leader, but he was getting *"old"* and his sons are wicked and corrupt. In spite of Samuel's positive upbringing and example, his kids turn out rotten. He is a national leader but anguishes over that his *"sons do not follow"* in his ways. It is amazing how dysfunction in a single leader's family can influence the course of a nation for so many centuries to come.

The descent from Exodus to Egypt accelerated, though, when the people clamor for a king to succeed Samuel as their national leader. *"We wanna king, we wanna king!"* Samuel understands this to be a direct rejection of God as their leader. The prophet lays into the people with the longest diatribe in the Old Testament about what a king will do to the people (vv. 10-17). Essentially, he says that a king will take your children, crops, livelihood, and pour it all into his war machine. You'll be slaves and return to pre-Exodus condition. You'll pray but God won't answer (v. 18).

Why, then, do the people insist on a king? Because they clamor to be governed *"like other nations"* (v. 5). Wrong hopes, wrong model, and wrong outcome. God let them choose their own foolish path, and Israel got exactly what she wished for – and it led to her ruin.

A succession crisis, family dysfunction, emulating the wrong example ... throw a dart and you will hit on a cause for the demise of God's promising experiment with a nation.

1 SAMUEL 14

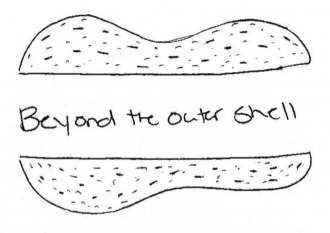

Beyond the outer Shell

"Cast the lot between me and my son Jonathan." And Jonathan was taken." – 1 Samuel 14:42

The pictures of King Saul and his son Jonathan in 1 Samuel 14 offers a study in contrasts. Younger Jonathan shows faith and humility: *"come, let us go over (to the enemy) ... it may be that the Lord will act for us; for nothing can hinder the Lord from saving by many or by few" (v. 6)*. Older Saul, on the other hand, shows a fear-based, misguided piety and leadership: *"Now Saul committed a very rash act on that day. He laid an oath on the troops ..." (v. 24)*.

Jonathan comes off as daring, winsome, faithful. Saul is portrayed as fearful, too careful, and misguided.

At the end of the day, a picture of holy leadership comes into focus. Leadership is not about outward signs of piety. Saul casts lots (v. 19), builds altars (v. 34), makes sacred oaths (v. 24) – and fails to lead. Jonathan shows faith (v. 6), courage (v. 13), honesty, and humility (v. 43). He won the hearts of the people (v. 45), accomplished the victory over the Philistines, and foreshadowed the heart of David, the greatest model of leadership for Israel.

Prayer: *Lord, grant today the grace for me to lead from the inside out and not according to hollow outward rituals. Please give the strength of character to do what is right, to be a thermostat rather than a thermometer. In the name of Jesus, who was obedient to you in a way that was beyond how others assessed him, Amen.*

John P. Chandler

I SAMUEL 15

WHEN NOT TO LISTEN
TO OTHERS

"The word of the Lord came to Samuel: "I regret that I made Saul king, for he has turned back from following me, and has not carried out my commands." – I Samuel 15:10-11

Though Saul wins a great victory over his enemies in 1 Samuel 15, by the end of this chapter he is broken and made into a lame duck king. Both God and Samuel grieved this disappointment (v. 35). How is it that Saul won the battle but lost the war?

The crux seems to be in Saul's failure to listen and completely carry out the holy instructions of Samuel (and the Lord) to "*utterly destroy*" Amalek (v. 3). Instead, Saul spared King Agag (pity? Hope for a ransom) and some of the best sheep, ostensibly "to sacrifice to the Lord" (v. 15). But the story tells us more about motive: Saul has "*set up a monument for himself*" (v. 12). Moreover, Saul has committed a "*rebellion*" (v. 23) against God by once again preferring the voice of the people: "*I have transgressed the commandment of the Lord and your words, because I feared the people and obeyed their voice*" (v. 24).

There is a time for leaders to listen carefully to what the people call for, and to serve them by giving them what they want. But in other instances, such as this one, to do so is to betray leadership. In the end, "the Lord has torn the kingdom from (Saul) and has given it to a neighbor of yours, who is better than you" (v. 28). We know this new leader to be David – a man after God's own heart.

Prayer: *Lord, please give us the courage to know when to listen to those over whom we have been given charge, and when to serve them by refusing to listen. We pray for the heart and spirit of your wisdom to fill our ears. In the name of Jesus, Amen.*

John P. Chandler   73

1 SAMUEL 16–17

HEIGHT VERSUS HEART

"But the Lord said to Samuel, "Do not look upon his appearance or the height of his stature ... for the Lord does not see as mortals see; they look upon the outward appearance, but the Lord looks on the heart."
– 1 Samuel 16:7

Malcolm Gladwell in *Blink* mused on why North Americans prefer tall leaders. While only three percent of the general U.S. population are 6' 2" or taller, thirty percent of Fortune 500 CEOs are. Of our unconscious prejudice, Gladwell says,

"Have you ever wondered why so many mediocrities find their way into positions of authority in companies and organizations? It's because when it comes to even the most important positions, we think that our selection decisions are a good deal more rational than they actually are. We see a tall person, and we swoon."

It's not a new problem. The first king of Israel, Saul, was a reluctant and deeply disturbed tragic figure whose life ended in suicide and whose reign was disastrous. So how did a man like Saul ever get to be king? *"There was not a man among the people of Israel more handsome than he; he stood head and shoulders above everyone else"* (9:2). Saul was tall.

This is why the story of David makes so much of the details that he was a youngest son and shepherd (16:11), a food courier and baggage keeper (17:17-18, 22), and a laughable youthful contrast *"disdained"* by the giant Goliath (17:41-44). I'm guessing David wasn't tall.

But *"the Lord does not save by sword and spear"* (v. 47), and God is not only looking for tall leaders. When Samuel is being guided by God to search for the next leader, he is explicitly told to reject *"appearance"* or *"height"* as criteria. *"For the Lord does not see as mortals see ... the Lord looks on the heart."*

When sizing people up for leadership, if we'd rather get David than Saul, we might consider the way of God, who values *"heart"* over *"height."*

1 SAMUEL 20

VITAL FRIENDS

"Jonathan made David swear again by his love for him; for he loved him as he loved his own life." – 1 Samuel 20:17

Author and Gallup pollster Tom Rath studied why some people get stuck in chronic homelessness while others are able to make their way out of it. The key and surprising difference? Those who thrived had formed vital and varied friendship networks. Rath extrapolates to posit that we'll live longer, healthier, more productive and successful lives when we do the same. He illustrates in his book *Vital Friends* the "Eight Vital Roles" that friends play in your life: "Builder, Champion, Collaborator, Companion, Connector, Energizer, Mind Opener and Navigator."

A surprising amount of attention in the biblical story of king David is devoted to his friendship with Jonathan. (There is, by the way, no suggestion that it was a sexual relationship, as some have speculated. The Bible was quick to condemn David's improper sexual relationship with Bathsheba in 2 Samuel 11 and would have been just as quick to do so if that were the case here.) Clearly, the friendship between the two men was life-giving, sustaining, and a source of strength in difficult times for David's life and leadership. David was never so busy as a leader that he did not have time for investing in and receiving from his best friend, Jonathan.

In like manner, Jesus had not only twelve close disciples but also three closest friends among them (Peter, James, and John). The biblical pattern is an important corrective for leaders who believe they can maximize their potential simply by working all the time, disregarding the core-life investments in the relational capital of friendship. We are wise leaders when we intentionally cultivate close friendships.

Exercise: *Do a personal audit of Rath's eight types of friendships. Which of the eight types of friends do you have, and which do you lack? Thank God for the friends you have ... and ask God to give you eyes for the friends you don't yet have, but need in your life.*

---

1 SAMUEL 28

RESORTING TO SUPERSTITION

"When Saul inquired of the Lord, the Lord did not answer him, not by dreams, or by Urim, or by prophets. Then Saul said to his servants, "Seek out for me a woman who is a medium, so that I may go to her and inquire of her."
– 1 Samuel 28:6-7

This scene describes the tragic, pathetic end to a tall king's life. What began with such high hopes is now ending with a trembling king (v. 5), in disguise (v. 8), in the tent of the very sort of astrologer he had officially banned as ungodly (v. 9). He prays and there is no answer. He is about to step onto a battlefield where his sons will be killed and he will fall on his own sword in suicide and disgrace (v. 19). How did such a promising leader fall so far, so fast?

The explanation for his downfall is that Saul *"did not obey the voice of the Lord"* (v. 18). In 1 Samuel 13-15, Saul repeatedly had taken matters into his own hands, foolishly offering the sacrifice instead of waiting for the priest Samuel to do so. Why the impulsivity, impatience, and impetuousness? Why risk the wrath of God through such an offensive ritual violation?

He did so because *"the people began to slip away from Saul"* (13:8). And the king cared so much of what people thought of him, that he increasingly *"committed very rash acts"* (14:24). He began a habit of pandering to public opinion and listening to the crowd. It ultimately resulted in giving away his soul as a leader. He crouches in a tent, asking a witch to tell him what to do.

Over-concern for public opinion and a high need to guide it mix a recipe for resorting to superstition. Nancy Reagan infamously set presidential travel plans based on horoscopes, but she was neither the first or last to lean on fortune-tellers. We can head down a path of depending on ridiculous superstition for guidance when we care so much about what people say that we forget to care even more about what God says.

1 SAMUEL 30

FROM WARRIOR TO KING

"David was in great danger; for the people spoke of stoning him, because all the people were bitter in spirit for their sons and daughters. But David strengthened himself in the Lord his God." – 1 Samuel 30:6

In 1 Samuel 30, David the leader is in danger of being stoned by his own people. They blame him for the loss of their families. He survives the crisis because he "strengthened himself in the Lord" (v. 6). After showing hospitality to an Egyptian straggler who provides him with an incredible intelligence report (vv. 11-15), David the warrior then leads to a military victory and recovers not only the lost families but additional spoil. What happens next is critical. Upon his return, those who fought wish to exclude the spoils of victory from the exhausted comrades who stayed behind. But controversially, David refused, saying, "For the share of the one who goes down into the battle shall be the same as the share of the one who stays by the baggage; they shall share alike" (v. 24). David goes on to offer "presents" from the spoil to other friends as well (v. 26).

Here is the evolution from David as a mere <u>warrior</u> to David as <u>king</u>. It takes valiance to risk fighting a just and dangerous battle. But it takes another kind of wisdom for a leader to insist on a community not simply governed by force and power, but which remembers and provides for the exhausted ones left behind by the stronger.

Prayer: Dear Lord who always remembers "the least of these," the stranger, the weak: make us ready to fight when that is the righteous thing to do. But make us also ready to share when that is unpopular. We strengthen ourselves in you when we are tried in the court of public opinion. And we pray for the clarity from you to govern not as mere mighty warriors, but as wise rulers. In the name of Jesus, Amen.

John P. Chandler

2 SAMUEL 2

"Is the sword to keep devouring forever? Do you not know that the end will be bitter? How long will it be before you order your people to turn from the pursuit of their kinsmen?"
– 2 Samuel 2:26

After the death of Saul, David mourns appropriately (1:17-27), prays for guidance (2:1-3), and begins his reign with an offer of friendship to his would-be rivals (4-7). But Saul and David's generals, Abner and Joab, begin a *"contest"* (v. 14), something like a tournament – and it rapidly degenerates into a real and serious military conflict, embodied by the killing of Asahel by Abner (vv. 18-24).

The only way that battle does not turn into all-out war is that Abner finally calls out to Joab, *"Is the sword to keep devouring forever? Do you now know that the end will be bitter? How long will it be before you order your people to turn from the pursuit of their kinsmen?"* (v. 26) After that, there is a truce (vv. 27f).

The encounter between these two generals shows leadership at its worst and best. At its worst, these leaders allowed a contest to escalate to true and lethal hostility. At its best, they pulled the plug on a battle and contained the harm.

Leaders know when to break a circuit of escalation and how to do damage control. Generals Abner and Joab would have done well to follow the example of King David, who began with *"inquiring of the Lord"* (v.1) and offering friendship to former enemies (vv. 4-7).

Prayer*: Lord, give me the grace as a leader today not to allow hostile rhetoric and risky games to degenerate and escalate into something far worse. Give me the grace to step into the middle of heated conflict and break the circuits that can only lead to pain. In the name of Jesus who did these things, Amen.*

---

2 SAMUEL 3

HONORING YOUR COMPETITION

"There was a long war between the house of Saul and the house of David; David grew stronger and stronger, while the house of Saul became weaker and weaker." – 2 Samuel 3:1

Second Samuel 3:1 is a working out of the report that *"the house of David grew stronger and stronger"*; the rest of the chapter bears out how that shift came to be. Much of it was through David's shrewd leadership, which transcended revenge and blood-feuds. David welcomes a proposed alliance with Joab, general of his deceased rival (Saul) and heir-through-coup to an opposing tribe in the North that David must win over in order to consolidate power. Abner (David's general), however, has a feud with Joab (escalated from chapter 2) and murders him.

David could have gloated over the death of his most powerful rival, but instead rebukes his right-hand-man Joab for the murder. He honors Abner as a *"prince and great man,"* and publicly mourns in the equivalent of a media event. The result is that *"All the people took notice of it, and it pleased them; just as everything the king did pleased all the people"* (v. 36).

Great leadership fundamentally unites rivals and transcends resistance. As David sensitively honored an opponent, he demonstrated that his rule would be greater than cycles of tribal warrior retaliation and triumph by might.

Prayer: *Lord, just as Jesus taught us to love our enemies and pray for those who persecute us, let us learn to recognize the fundamental humanity of even those who oppose us. Even as we might be called to defeat people, let us know how not to crush them utterly. Give us the wisdom to honor our rivals in the great work of unity and community.*

John P. Chandler

2 SAMUEL 6

RECOVERING

"They brought in the ark of the Lord, and set it in its place, inside the tent that David had pitched for it; and David offered burnt offerings and offerings of well-being before the Lord. When David had finished offering the burnt offerings and the offerings of well-being, he blessed the people in the name of the Lord of hosts, and distributed food among all the people ..."– 2 Samuel 6:17-19

In I Samuel 6, David is trying to consolidate opposing factions (from the house of predecessor Saul) in Jerusalem, a new city, and to make this city a religious (as well as political and military) center. His ability to gather fragmented tribes represents the height of Israel's power; for one shining moment, Israel (and not the Egyptian, Assyrian, Philistine, or Babylonian empires) was at the center and pinnacle of rule in the Middle East.

How did this happen? Beyond military victory (I Samuel 5) and skillful political maneuvering (I Samuel 3-4), David united and captured the hearts of disparate people by importing the Ark of the Covenant into Jerusalem. Having lay dormant for twenty years (I Samuel 4-6), the ark is brought, with peril and in small steps, into Jerusalem. There is mighty joy and dancing at this event. The lone dissenting voice (Michal, vv. 16-23) is notably out of touch with the vast majority who affirm the return of the ark to the center of the community.

From a leadership perspective, this move was brilliant: David imaginatively invigorates conservative holdovers from previous regimes by elevating the very symbol of their elemental faith in God. The ark is the taproot of the old Israel's religious vitality. By bringing it joyously to Jerusalem, David is assuring those whose lives have been gathered around it that they have a place in this city.

Leaders can achieve unity through honoring the deep and honorable symbols of those with whom they disagree – and, where they are able to agree with what is affirmed through those symbols, they do so with joy and dancing (vv. 5, 14f).

John P. Chandler

2 SAMUEL 11

PUTTING YOURSELF IN A POSITION TO FAIL

"In the spring of the year, the time when kings go out to battle, David sent Joab with his officers and all Israel with him; they ravaged the Ammonites, and besieged Rabbah. But David remained at Jerusalem. It happened, late one afternoon, when David rose from his couch and was walking about on the roof of the king's house, that he saw from the roof a woman bathing; the woman was very beautiful."
– 2 Samuel 11:1-2

Praying the Kings

At the height of his power and from the height of his rooftop, David sets into motion events that led to pain for himself and to many generations beyond himself. David will imperil himself, his family, and the nation.

We should have seen it coming; after the great victory of chapter 10, David (for the first time) makes no attempt to thank God for victory. And now, in *"the time when kings go out to battle,"* when he should have been busy at work leading his people, king David was instead lounging in his home. The combination of getting a bit too proud and being a bit too bored was a cocktail for trouble.

The events that follow with his seduction (rape?) of Bathsheba and murder of her faithful warrior husband Uriah are like a laundry list of sins. Which of the Ten Commandments does David not break? He has been a spectacular leader, and here he has a spectacular fall. And his fall hurts not only himself; a baby dies, a marriage is shattered, an army is disrupted, and family dysfunction follows the house of David for the rest of his life. Eventually, even the stability of the nation is rocked. Who says that what we do in the bedroom is only our own business?

It is a sobering tale, and wise is the leader who learns from David's mistakes. (Immature leaders are limited only to learn from their own experience; the wise learn from the experiences of others.) A central lesson pertains to how David put himself at risk when his ego got too big and he slacked off of his leadership assignment, resulting in too much leisure time. In the words of Saint Jerome, his idle hands were the devil's workshop. Whatever tempts us most, we are wise to know it. And we are wise not to put ourselves in those danger zones where we are likely to unravel much or all of what we have worked for.

John P. Chandler

2 SAMUEL 14

WISE FRIENDS AND
RECONCILIATION

"For it was your servant Joab who commanded me; it was he who put all these words into the mouth of your servant. In order to change the course of affairs your servant Joab did this." – 2 Samuel 14:19-20

In 2 Samuel 14, we are told of the work of David's right-hand-man, Joab, and a "wise woman" (v. 2) he enlists to bring about the reconciliation of king David and his beloved but estranged son, Absalom. Joab and this woman conspire for the good of the king and kingdom; this is in concert with God, who "will devise plans so as not to keep an outcast banished forever from his presence" (v. 14).

In the end, David only partly accepted the wise scheming of his friends Joab and this unnamed woman to effect reconciliation. David only partly welcomed Absalom home, and his refusal to pardon his son fully eventually led to his son revolting to the point of leading an all-out civil war. Delaying reconciliation is costly.

But in the meantime, there are things for leaders to learn from the efforts of those around them who wish to give potentially life-changing help. "In order to change the course of affairs your servant Joab did this," said the wise woman (v. 20). It is up the king to act on this wisdom. But would that every leader – and every family – be blessed with intervening friends and servants whose heart is to help others get through brokenness and impasse through story and intervention.

Prayer: *God, grant us the wisdom to hear in the voices of loving friends the counsel that will lead to wholeness. Give us the stories that transform bureaucratic stuck-ness and move us to renewal of what is noble and right and beautiful. In Jesus' name, Amen.*

John P. Chandler   91

2 SAMUEL 15

THE COSTS OF
DELAYED RECONCILIATION

*"Absalom would say, "See, your claims are good and right;
but there is no one deputed by the king to hear you ... If
only I were judge in the land!" – 2 Samuel 15:3-4*

In 2 Samuel 14, Joab and a wise woman engineer a reunion of estranged son Absalom with his father, King David. They put both parties in a position of achieving reconciliation. But instead, there is a kind of uneasy détente, where Absalom is welcomed back to town but not to the king's house. *"So Absalom lived two full years in Jerusalem without coming into the king's presence"* (14:28). Later, the two meet (14:33), but the damage is done.

The story of chapter 15 reveals the damage done by delayed reconciliation. Absalom has stewed for years and carefully *"stole the hearts of the people of Israel"* (v. 6). Never mind that he did so through false promises (1-6), betrayal, and religious pretext (7-12); the conspiracy results in David's own Passion Narrative, departure into the wilderness, Gethsemane (v. 30) and eventually the final and costly rupture of relationship with his beloved first-born.

Chickens have come home to roost in this sad story:

> ⤜ David's own folly with Bathsheba is now (as predicted in 12:10) playing out in next-generation family discord;

> ⤜ David's failures to administer justice now give opportunity for Absalom to exploit popular sentiment;

> ⤜ And maybe most of all, David's indecisiveness, passivity, and cluelessness now escalate to where "home" issues are playing themselves out in a very public arena – to the great cost of the nation.

David and those around him will pay a great price because of failing to pursue actively the possibility of reconciliation when that opportunity became available. Not only does a son become an enemy, but a whole nation pays.

Prayer: *Lord, as my friends in recovery pray, grant to me the ability to make a fearless, searching, moral inventory today. And if there are places where I am not reconciled as I should be, give me eyes to seek opportunities to do so, and courage not to delay that reconciliation. In the name of Jesus, Amen.*

John P. Chandler   93

2 SAMUEL 17

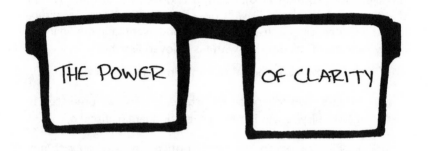

"For the Lord had ordained to defeat the good counsel of Ahithophel, so that the Lord might bring ruin to Absalom."
– 2 Samuel 17:14

The story of Absalom's failed rebellion against his father David's rule is ultimately a story of God's choosing and providence. The Lord worked in a variety of circumstances to "bring ruin on Absalom" (v. 14). Ultimately history is determined neither by the rational positivism of human agency alone, nor a romantic supernaturalism of God acting independently from people (Walter Brueggemann). God and leaders collaborate well or poorly, and so goes human history.

One way leaders work well or poorly with God is in regard to whom they listen to and how. Second Samuel 17 describes Absalom's decision to go with the wrong counselor. Ahithophel's advice to Absalom is straightforward, intelligent, timely, and doesn't escalate a volatile situation. Naturally, Absalom asks for a second opinion! When he does, he gets one – a bad one. But Hushai's plan plays on Absalom's ego; it is grandiose and complicated, and it ends up buying David badly-needed time to escape and mobilize. God, of course, is working beneath the surface: *"for the Lord had ordained to defeat the good counsel of Ahithophel"* (v. 14).

Alongside of providence, though, there is something for the leader to learn about wise counsel, and that is this: clarity is a rare and prized treasure. Clarity is not the same as simplicity and does not mean humans have no responsibility. The Lord *"will make straight your paths"* (Proverbs 3:6) but we still have to walk them. But when leaders are tempted with windy, wordy, indecipherable advice, they cut through the ego of those plans and march in step with the clear straight ways of God's leading.

2 SAMUEL 18

Hanging between Heaven and Earth
without a mule

"His head caught fast in the oak, and he was left hanging between heaven and earth, while the mule that was under him went on." – 2 Samuel 18:9

The climax of the national conflict between David and Absalom comes to a head, and yet the biblical report focuses on the inner ambivalence of the characters. Ahimaaz the messenger is alternately bold (v. 19) and cowardly (v. 29). Joab is loyal (v. 2), yet disregards royal orders (vv. 11-15). Most of all, King David is leader of an army (vv. 1-4), but is preoccupied with being the father of a son (vv. 5, 30-33). His grief over the death of his rebel son outweighs his feelings of victory as a commander in chief.

Perhaps the richest metaphor for this ambivalence lies in the description of Absalom's entrapment in the forest. As *"the mule went under the thick branches of a great oak,"* the long-haired rebel *"caught fast in the oak, and* **he was left hanging between heaven and earth while the mule that was under him went on"** (v. 9).

What a picture! Absalom, in this liminal state, is between life and death, both rebel and son. Perhaps it is a reminder that people are more complex than their position. We are a hot mess of outer actions and inner conflicts, official roles and being somebody's parent. God, give us grace to do what we must do as leaders even though our guts are clenched with ambivalence! And give us grace to recognize the humanity even in our enemies.

2 SAMUEL 23

THE GREATNESS OF GREATNESS THROUGH OTHERS

"These are the names of the warriors whom David had ..."
– 2 Samuel 23:8

Second Samuel 23 attempts to summarize the legacy of David. Interestingly, the stories it tells are mostly about the exploits of those around him. One describes Shammah, who "*took his stand*" in battle through which "*the Lord brought about a great victory*" (v. 12). Another is about Benaiah, who "*killed a lion in a pit on a day when snow had fallen*" (v. 20). These are stories of David's "*mighty men,*" namely "*the Three*" and "*the Thirty*" – his inner circle of co-leaders.

This is telling. David's last leadership legacy was that:

a) The story speaks of the exploits of David's <u>team</u> as much as if not more than those of David; and

b) David's greatness is shown in his solidarity with his soldiers.

There are so many things that can be drawn from this, including the ideas that:

➶ David didn't monopolize credit.

➶ The nation of Israel is greater than even the great man David.

➶ No ruler rules without great and loyal people around him.

➶ Every leader must be surrounded by a "*Three*" and "*Thirty*" – strategically chosen circles of valiant, strong leaders whose exploits are noteworthy in and of themselves, but who subvert ego to a great cause beyond themselves.

➶ Nation trumps leader, and God trumps nation!

Jesus had his twelve disciples, and within them, the three (Peter, James, and John). Among your closest co-leaders, who is in your innermost circle?

John P. Chandler   99

1 KINGS 3

WISE LEADERSHIP

"And now, O Lord my God, you have made your servant king ... although I am only a little child. And your servant is in the midst of the people whom you have chosen, a great people, so numerous that they cannot be numbered or counted. Give your servant therefore an understanding mind to govern your people, able to discern between good and evil; for who can govern this your great people?"
— I Kings 3:7-9

Wisdom is an instinct for the truth, the ability to see things on earth as they are in heaven. The story of King Solomon receiving and exercising wisdom rich illustrates how rulers receive the gift of wisdom from God and use it. It is helpful to look at the framework for how a leader gains wisdom:

1. As a <u>servant</u> (the word is used four times in vv. 6-9);

2. As a <u>covenant partner</u> with God (vv. 6, 14);

3. Is framed with the leader offering great personal <u>sacrifice</u>, generosity, worship, and prayer (vv. 4, 15);

4. Begins in a <u>dream</u>, remembering, and in a history greater than any one person (like Joseph in Genesis 41);

5. With a goal of the <u>welfare</u> of the people (v. 8);

6. Characterized by faithfulness, <u>discernment</u>, and righteousness;

7. Gained through "<u>asking</u>" (Solomon asks God 8 times in chapter 3);

8. Provides <u>justice for all</u> – even women prostitutes and unnamed children (vv. 16-28);

9. Is about the <u>mission</u> of the people, not the agenda of an individual (v. 9); and

10. Is <u>uncontaminated</u> by unlimited power.

Leaders are givers, dreamers, askers, deciders, worshipers.

A leader can do no better than the prayer of Solomon himself (vv. 7-9):

> And now, O Lord my God, you have made your servant king ... although I am only a little child. And your servant is in the midst of the people whom you have chosen, a great people, so numerous that they cannot be numbered or counted. Give your servant therefore an understanding mind to govern your people, able to discern between good and evil; for who can govern this your great people?"

John P. Chandler

1 KINGS 4

FOOD AND WISDOM

"These officials supplied provisions for King Solomon and for all who came to King Solomon's table, each one in his month; they let nothing be lacking." – 1 Kings 4:27

First Kings 4 is a press-release summary of the pinnacle of Solomon's reign. (There is dark foreshadowing here with the mention of huge military forces and the taxation necessary to sustain them, but those stories will be filled out later.) For now, here is the description of the peak: *Judah and Israel were as numerous as the sand by the sea; they ate, drank, and were happy. Solomon was sovereign over all the kingdoms ... During Solomon's lifetime Judah and Israel lived in safety, from Dan even to Beer-sheba, all of them under their vines and fig trees* (vv. 20-21, 25).

Much of the description of peace and happiness in the land revolves around Solomon providing <u>food</u> and <u>wisdom</u> (vv. 29ff). Not just food for those in power (v. 7, 22f), but so that **all** (even the poor) "*have their vines and fig trees."* And not just wisdom solely for his own national interests, but the kind of wisdom for which "*people came from all the nations to hear the wisdom of Solomon*" (vv. 34).

Solomon reached his peak as a leader when even the poor had enough to eat, and when his vast wisdom was not simply for building his own empire, but benefitted all the nations of the earth. He later (famously) lost this vision and became self-indulgent. The final enactment of wisdom and provision would have to wait. It would appear one thousand years later in the person of Jesus, of whom people would be "*astounded*" and say, "*Where did this man get all this? What is this wisdom that has been given to him? What deeds of power are being done by his hands! Is not this the son of Mary ...?*" (Mark 6:2-3).

The greatest (and most humble) leader of all time <u>fed</u> his people and embodied <u>wisdom</u>. Great leaders today do the same.

1 KINGS 5

ARE TEMPLES WISE?

"But now the Lord my God has given me rest on every side;
there is neither adversary nor misfortune ... So I intend to
build a house for the name of the Lord my God, as the Lord
said to my father David ... Therefore command that cedars
from the Lebanon be cut for me." – 1 Kings 5:4-6

Praying the Kings

This is beginning of King Solomon's downfall. God has given him *"wisdom"* (3:12) and *"shalom – rest on every side"* (v. 4). The nation is marked by:

➢ Security, stability, and harmony with neighbors (externally); and

➢ Abundance, prosperity, plentiful food, and justice for all (internally).

And while the official rhetoric is that the building of the temple is connected God's promise (v. 5), the writer makes it clear that the next things that happen with temple-building have to do with taxes and slavery:

➢ *"com*mand that cedars from the Lebanon be cut for me" (v. 6); and

➢ "King Solomon conscripted forced labor out of all Israel" (v. 13).

The temple is a religious symbol, a political statement, and a monument to Solomon's pride ("edifice complex!"). Building the temple was the height of Israel's nationhood – and the pedestal from which she fell.

One thousand years and much oppression later, as people again foolishly trusted their own buildings, Jesus would say, *"Destroy this temple, and in three days I will raise it up"* (John 2:19). After great public protest, the Gospel then notes, *"But he was speaking of the temple of his body"* (v. 21). And on Good Friday, his temple was destroyed.

Finally, for us, wisdom and shalom flow not from what temples we build, but from a temple broken for us. This temple results not in tax and slavery, but in an internal and external peace which is the hope of the world.

John P. Chandler   105

1 KINGS 9

"The Lord appeared to Solomon a second time, as he had appeared to him at Gibeon." – I Kings 9:2

We are not self-invented people. As scholar Walter Brueggemann puts is, "*We do not live by what we can make on our own. We live by the inscrutable surprises that come to us.*" And real joy comes when what we <u>want</u> to do is aligned with what these surprises tell us that we <u>must</u> do.

As with Joseph, Solomon is a leader whose life has been shaped by a dream. To live and lead well is to discern and live according to the dream that God has given us. It changes our life and can change the world. A leader must never get beyond or aside from this God-given dream. God is not mocked, and the story of Solomon never hesitates to connect disaster with sin. We do, but the Bible does not.

At the end of the day, the good news is that the dream of God for the world is finally shaped by the resurrection of Jesus Christ. The dream is that life conquers death, love overcomes evil, and the Lord reigns supreme over all the kings of the earth. The joyful cry is not only that "God is great!" It is also that "God is good!" And the dream of God is for the healing and repair of all creation.

1 KINGS 10

THE TRUE PURPOSE OF PROSPERITY AND WISDOM

"Blessed be the Lord your God, who has delighted in you and set you on the throne of Israel! Because the Lord loved Israel forever, he made you king to execute justice and righteousness." – 1 Kings 10:9

First Kings 10 describes the visit of the queen of Sheba (perhaps Yemen? Ethiopia?) to Solomon at the peak of his fame. She comes to engage in a contest of wits and to see all of the "stuff" – and is left breathless with amazement (v. 6). She is emblematic of a whole world which is dazzled by the prosperity of Solomon's court (v. 24).

But in the middle of her congratulatory speech, she makes a subtle and surprising statement, becoming, in effect, the mouthpiece for the narrator of the story: *"Because the Lord loved Israel forever, he has made you king to execute justice and righteousness" (v. 9)*.

This is prophetic. The queen is reminding Solomon to remember the covenant with God. The covenant connects **wisdom/prosperity** with **justice/righteousness**. Solomon, while amassing exotic and unparalleled treasure (*"apes and peacocks!"* – v. 22), seems to have forgotten that he has been given *"fame due to the name of the Lord"* (v. 2). And two chapters later, a resistance movement splits the kingdom and sends it spiraling into a decline from which it would never recover.

God gives leaders wisdom and prosperity not for their own gain and fame, but to execute justice and righteousness on behalf of others who have no voice. This was best embodied a millennium later: *"He is the source of your life in Christ Jesus, who became for us **wisdom from God, and righteousness** and sanctification and redemption ..."* (1 Corinthians 1:30). Jesus enacts wisdom. He is the model leader, in that what he did with his platform, he did on behalf of others, and not for himself.

Prayer: *Dear Lord, giver of all wisdom and prosperity, help me not to be flattered by the praise of others so that I forget that all that I have been given is a gift of your boundless generosity, and is not the work of my own ingenuity. Let me be not numbed by fame and deafened by riches until I become blind to the poor and tasteless in my disregard of justice. Give me the strength of Jesus to lead by serving for justice and righteousness, for the sake of your name, Amen.*

---

1 KINGS 12

The opposite of wisdom

"If you will be a servant to this people and serve them, and speak good words to them when you answer them, then they will be your servants forever." But he disregarded the advice that the older men gave him, and consulted with the young men who had grown up with him and now attended him."
– 1 Kings 12:7-8

Solomon is dead, having gone sour in the final chapter of his life, coaxed into poor rule by an unruly household. I Kings 12 tells of the undoing of *shalom* and dividing of the kingdom through the conflict of sons Rehoboam and Jeroboam. Theirs is the story of the opposite of wisdom (chapter 3, the beginning of Solomon's reign based in the dream of God and the divine gift of administering wisely).

Rehoboam asks for advice, and promptly listens to the wrong advisors, young men who mock the words of conciliation of older advisors. The older advisors had counseled the king to be a servant-leader: *"If you will be a servant to this people today and serve them, and speak good words to them when you answer them, then they will be your servants forever. But he disregarded the advice ..."* (vv. 7-8). He chose sadistic machismo over empathetic servanthood, and the kingdom split in rebellion over the choice.

Leaders are first <u>listeners</u> and <u>followers</u>. We loathe to admit that we are influenced by anyone, believing that we think independently and act autonomously. But every one of us has an invisible audience, a chorus of voices inside of us and around us. And the wise leader is the one who picks the right voices to heed and follow. Indeed, listening to the right voices around us is part of listening to the guidance of God himself.

Prayer: O Lord, in times of decision, grant to us the wisdom and clarity to sift, rank, and respond well to the voices in our ear. Help us to be good deciders because we have been good listeners and good servants. Make us discriminating listeners. And help our decisions to result in the creation of shalom and not its undoing. In the name of Jesus, Amen.

---

1 KINGS 13

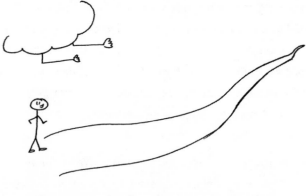

OBEDIENCE, NOT MOTIVE

"While Jeroboam was standing by the altar of incense, a man of God came out of Judah by the word of the Lord to Bethel and proclaimed against the altar by the word of the Lord ..."
– 1 Kings 13:1-2

The story of "*man of God*" and "*false prophet*" in I Kings 13 has confounded interpreters for ages. The man of God condemns wicked king Jeroboam for apostasy and the king's hand withers when it stretches out to attack the man of God. The man of God refuses a royal invitation to dine but is later tricked by a lying prophet (who knows why this second prophet would lie?). Ultimately, the man of God is killed by a God-sent lion because of unintentional disobedience to "*the word of the Lord*" (the key phrase in the story, found in vv. 1, 2, 5, 9, 17, 18). It turns out that seductive false religion is more dangerous to the prophet than royal power.

Search as you may, and you cannot uncover an unambiguous motive in the whole story. This story is about obedience, not motive. As Walter Brueggemann writes:

"The real point is a simple one: obey God's will. Do not quit on God's will because of royal protest. Do not turn back because of counter advice. Do not be taken in by the generous or hospitable, not by those who seem to have a deeper authority ... Attend to your call. Hold to it in spite of alternative possibilities. The text offers a radical notion of obedience, unflinching and undaunted by counter proposals."
(1 Kings, Knox Preaching Guides, pp. 67f.)

Too often, leaders are seduced by counter claims of power and authority. For the leader who has a call from God, the mandate is simple: obey the last clear thing you have heard from God, and continue to do so unless and until God speaks again.

Prayer: *O Lord, let us first, by the Holy Spirit, hear your voice – through the Bible, prayer, circumstances, the church. And then give us constancy of character, the backbone to adhere in obedience to your clear word. And help us not to be swayed by competing voices, for the sake of our call in Jesus Christ, Amen.*

John P. Chandler   113

1 KINGS 14

KING OR PROPHET?

*"... why do you pretend to be another? For I am charged
with heavy tidings for you." – 1 Kings 14:6*

In I Kings 14, the king Jeroboam's son falls sick, and he sends his wife, in disguise, to the blind prophet Ahijah. But the Lord speaks to the prophet – the Lord *always* speaks to the prophet – and the prophet says to the mother, "Why do you pretend to be another?" (v. 6). Ahijah prophesies doom to the child, the impious king, and an unfaithful nation, which ultimately comes to pass in the Babylonian Exile of 586 B.C. What follows in chapters 14-16 are brief summaries of the reign of kings as the nation splits and spirals to doom.

Friends from all over the world emailed me during the British royal wedding of Prince William and Catherine Middleton. Some described it as a historic event. But the Bible's account of I Kings 14-16 makes it clear that the real movers of history are not royal persons at all. Kings like Jeroboam, Abijah, Asa, Nadab, Baasha, Elah, Zimri, Omri ... they come and go as minor footnotes. What truly abide are the words of the prophets, who point to obedience or disobedience to God as the true shaper of history.

The wise leader understands that heads of state are finally evaluated not by their position vis-à-vis other nations, but by how they relate to the prophetic word. We're not graded on a curve. We're not defined by political or national alliances. We're ultimately assessed by obedience to God.

1 KINGS 17

PUNISHMENT OR PREPARATION?

"The ravens brought him bread and meat in the morning, and bread and meat in the evening; and he drank from the wadi. But after a while the wadi dried up, because there was no rain in the land." – 1 Kings 17:6-7

Elijah bursts onto the scene in 1 Kings 17 without introduction. After several chapters on the merry-go-round, with ineffective, sinful kings, the end result is a pervasive and deeply symbolic drought and famine. How good is royal power when no one has anything to eat or drink?

But the book of "Kings" is really not about kings; it is finally about "Prophets." Because only the prophets are the ones sent by God who can finally say, "Do not be afraid" (v. 13), "the jar of meal will not be emptied" (v. 14), and "O Lord my God, let this child's life come into him again" (v. 21). The Lord listens to prophets. Kings? Not so much.

One other word about prophets: they must go into the wilderness (v. 3), into hostile territory, and depend on the "daily bread" of provision from God. Elijah does so and is fed bread and meat twice (!) daily – rich fare indeed, echoing the Exodus provision of manna and quail to the people of God. He drinks from the brook.

And then the brook dries up (v. 7)! A prophet must remember, though, that this is not punishment from God; it is preparation for later works. And because Elijah trusts God when the brook dries up, he is able to go from there and do greater things for the Lord, feeding widows and reviving dead children.

Leaders use hardship as a way of hardening their commitment to their holy calling.

1 KINGS 18

METHODICAL, PRAYERFUL LEADERSHIP

"Then Elijah said to all the people, "Come closer to me"; and all the people came closer to him. First he repaired the altar of the Lord that had been thrown down ..." – **1 Kings 18:30**

The confrontation in I Kings 18 between the prophet Elijah and king Ahab has often been portrayed in ways that emphasize the dramatic and miraculous. There has been a terrible drought – symbol of the king's ineffectiveness – and Ahab has been busy looking for animal food (v. 5) instead of solving the problems of starving widow (17:8-16). Elijah, called a "troubler" (for what? Feeding widows?!), connects drought and apostasy. In a well-known scene, Elijah takes on 450 royal prophets of Baal. (Interestingly, Baal was a fertility god ... and there was no rain. Hmmm.) The king's lackey-prophets dance and cut themselves in a great public show, but to no avail. Fire comes from heaven and answers Elijah (v. 38), Yahweh is vindicated (v. 39), and rain comes in fulfillment of the prophet's word (vv. 1, 41-45).

An overlooked aspect of leadership in this scene is found in Elijah's preparation of the altar. The false prophets hastily set up their altar and spend most of their time making a grand public spectacle (vv. 26-28) – to no avail. Elijah, on the other hand, is meticulous and methodical in his preparation. He whispers, repairs, rebuilds, conducts rituals repeatedly (vv. 30-35). There is no public showboating or charismatic miracle-working. There is a rigorous attentiveness, a simple prayer, and a divine response.

God often works through the methodical, prayerful, well-prepared work of a leader. It is often not dramatic. But it often works, because it places the spotlight off of oneself and onto the place where it belongs: the need for rain to relieve the drought and meet the needs of the people.

Prayer: *God, let my ego never get in the way of what needs to be done for your people. Help me to rely more on preparation than personal charisma. And help me to be thorough, well-prepared, courageous, and prayerful in waiting on you to do what only you can do, after I have done all that I can do. In the name of Jesus, Amen.*

John P. Chandler

1 KINGS 19

DEPRESSION

AND

RE-COMMISSIONING

"Then the word of the Lord came to him, saying, "What are you doing here, Elijah?" – 1 Kings 19:9

Far too much attention has been placed on the *"still, small voice"* (1 Kings 19:12) line of this chapter. Perhaps this is due to American individualism or our harried existence. But this is decidedly not the Bible's focal point of the story.

The story focuses instead on the <u>depression</u> and <u>re-commissioning</u> of a leader. Elijah, fresh off of a great victory over the prophets of Baal at Mount Carmel, is now extremely vulnerable and is terrified at a (relatively insignificant) threat from Queen Jezebel. He wants to give up his prophetic office. So he wanders into the wilderness, afraid, alone, and hungry. An angel of the Lord instructs him to eat and sleep, eat and sleep. (Oh, by the way, God provides food miraculously for him!) In the strength of that provision, Elijah goes to Mount Horeb (Sinai), where tradition said the Law was revealed to Moses. But Elijah withdraws into a cave.

At that point, *"the word of the Lord came to him saying, "What are you doing here, Elijah?"* (v. 9). This is God's re-commissioning of Elijah to his prophetic office. It's not divine fireworks – earthquake, wind, and fire – that draws Elijah out of the cave, but sheer silence. At that point, God tells Elijah to anoint two kings, and anoint his prophetic successor, Elijah. God also points out that Elijah is not as alone as he thinks he is: *"Yet I will leave seven thousand in Israel, all the knees that have not bowed to Baal"* (v. 18). The call from God is not only mystical and personal; it is also communal and incarnate.

There are factors that can result in a leader's depression: fear, travel, aloneness, lack of sleep, poor eating, stress, and threat.

And there are factors of restoration that can lead to a re-commissioning of the leader's holy calling: enough sleep, the strength of food, being in places of revelation, and being part of community. Like Abraham Maslow's hierarchy of needs, these "Elijah Disciplines" are the bedrock of human needs that lie beneath the ability to hear God call. Disciplined leaders follow them so as to be positioned to receive revelation.

John P. Chandler   121

1 KINGS 21

PROPHETS INTRUDE

"Because you have sold yourself to do what is evil in the sight of the Lord, I will bring disaster on you ..."
– 1 Kings 21:20-21

The story of King Ahab and Queen Jezebel seizing Naboth's vineyard in 1 Kings 21 began as one of royal overpowering through manipulation of the legal system, all under the cloak of piety. The royals covet a man's ancestral field for a *"vegetable garden"* (v. 2 – which, in light of Deuteronomy 11:10, was a symbol for the Egyptian antithesis of the Promised Land!). Naboth refuses on legal, moral, and family grounds. The royals sulk, then seize, cunningly twisting the Law. Naboth is "legally" killed and Ahab sets out to possess the field (v. 16).

Too often, the story ends at this point. But, *"Then the word of the Lord came to Elijah"* (v. 17). God has sent his prophets to lead in the face of power. *"Ahab said to Elijah, "Have you found me, O my enemy?" He answered, "I have found you. Because you have sold yourself to do what is evil in the sight of the Lord, I will bring disaster on you"* (vv. 20f). Kings come and go – and they "go" sooner when they violate and twist the just law of God in acts of covetousness, greed, and seizing.

History begins when prophets intrude. Hitler may annex Poland, but prophets like Dietrich Bonhoeffer pronounce that God is not mocked. The real leaders in history are not royals with titles; the real leaders are prophets, those who speak justice on behalf of the overpowered.

Prayer: *Lord, grant me this day eyes to see the least of these, and to hear the cry of the oppressed. Give me the courage to speak truth to power when power is evil. Cause me to see beyond national interests and into the higher law of what is right in your sight. In the name of Jesus, who died for doing so, but whose death redeemed, Amen.*

John P. Chandler   123

1 KINGS 22

LYING PROPHETS

"The messenger who had gone to summon Micaiah said to him, "Look, the words of the prophets with one accord are favorable to the king; let your word be like the word of one of them, and speak favorably." But Micaiah said, "As the Lord lives, whatever the Lord says to me, that I will speak."
– 1 Kings 22:13-14

How can a king hear the truth of a prophet when the prophet has bad news for him?

Ahab, a wicked king who thinks of himself as an autonomous ruler, surrounds himself with court prophets, "*about four hundred of them*" (v. 5). He would have gone into battle without asking anyone, but the more pious king and comrade Jehoshaphat insisted on inquiring on God's guidance first. Thus the cynical Ahab insists that if you have to have religion in the mix, at least it will be <u>my</u> religion. His 400 prophets, knowing who butters their bread, predict Ahab's victory. And Ahab intentionally excludes the counsel of prophet Micaiah. Ahab says, "*I hate him, for he never prophesies anything favorable about me, but only disaster*" (v. 8). The rest of the story is that the true prophet Micaiah gets his royal audience, and his predicted royal disaster comes to pass with the inglorious death of Ahab. (By the way, for his trouble, Micaiah gets slapped, thrown in prison, starved, and is never heard from again. One does not always get rich and popular from being a prophet.)

Leaders cannot be governed by the winds of public opinion or by "bought prophets." It can be painful to have truth-tellers around. But godly leaders want to hear divinely-guided counsel. They will slow down their plans long enough to hear from God – and be wise enough to change their course when they receive true prophetic advice to do so.

Prayer: *Lord, remind me that history is governed in the counsel of the Almighty, not by autonomous rulers. Help me to discern the true prophet from the false prophet. Tune my compass to the true north of your providence. In the name of Jesus, Amen."*

John P. Chandler

2 KINGS 1

PROPHETS > KINGS?

"So the third captain of fifty went up and came and fell on his knees before Elijah and entreated him ..." – 2 Kings 1:13

"We must obey God rather than any human authority" – Acts 5:29

The second book of Kings picks right up where the first book left off: it is really more of a story of prophets than it is of kings. King Ahaziah has fallen and he can't get up. Moab has rebelled, and because of his injury, the king is helpless to respond. As a son of Jezebel, Ahaziah instinctively turns to Baal-zebub for an oracle to help. (A footnote – this name, later used in the New Testament as a name for Satan (*Beelzebub*), was a mocking pun; it turned "Lord of Princes" into "Lord of Flies" or the "manure pile!"). People under pressure are always looking for oracles and can be a bit indiscriminate about where they look for them!

So Ahaziah summons the prophet Elijah. The king thinks he's in charge of the prophet and so he "*sends*" for him. But in each of the first two commands, the prophet calls down fire from heaven and consumes the king's summoners, fifty-plus each time. Finally the king's captain "*fell on his knees before Elijah and entreated him*" (v. 13). This is the more proper way for an inferior to address a superior.

And thus the point of the story is made. Kings may rule nations, but prophets are greater than kings. As commentator Richard Nelson writes, "*The Christian church must always remember that "thus says the king" never takes precedence over "thus says the Lord"* (Acts 4:19f, 5:27-29). The wise leader knows that s/he may be given a domain to rule, but that his or her word falls under the Word of the Lord as made alive in the mouth of messengers sent by God.

Prayer: *O Lord, you have granted me power – but never let me act outside of the authority you have granted me. Attune my ears to the words of your prophets, your messengers, who speak truth, so that I may lead in concert with your revelation. In the name of Jesus, Amen."*

---

2 KINGS 2

PASSING THE MANTLE

*"When they had crossed, Elijah said to Elisha, "Tell me what
I may do for you, before I am taken from you." Elisha said,
"Please let me inherit a double share of your spirit." He
responded, "You have asked for a hard thing …"*
– 2 Kings 2:9-10

It is time for the prophet Elijah to exit the stage. He, not the kings, has been the locus of transforming hope for the nation. But his chapter is over, as it will end one day for all of us. And it is now time for the next prophet (Elisha) to enter the stage and speak the word of transforming hope.

There is a testing of Elisha, followed by declarations of willingness to take on the hard work of his predecessor, and miraculous confirming signs. (Both Elijah and Elisha part the water because, like Moses, prophetic leadership is always about liberation from oppression and crossing over into a new and free land). Finally, the community exclaims, *"The spirit of Elijah rests on Elisha"* (v. 15). And Elisha then performs miracles (clearing up bad water, vv. 19-22) and pronounces fiery judgment (vv. 23-24) in the same manner as the one who had come before him.

In this, we see leadership that <u>passes the mantle</u>. It looks like this:
> a. I do it.
> b. I do it and you are with me.
> c. You do it and I am with you.
> d. You do it.
> e. You do it and someone else is with you.

We have not finished our prophetic task until we have passed on to another who can do what we did and say what we said – and then some.

Thanks be to Jesus Christ, who saw fit to invest his earthly life in mentoring twelve ordinary people, and in so doing, passed the mantle that rests on us today!

Exercise: *In whom are you investing your life? Who is a person to whom you could or should "pass the mantle?" Pray that God would make clear to you who these people might be.*

John P. Chandler   129

2 KINGS 3

PROSE AND MUSIC,
KING AND PROPHET

"And then, while the musician was playing, the power of the Lord came on him. And he said, "Thus says the Lord, 'I will make this wadi full of pools." – 2 Kings 3:15-16

Praying the Kings

The kings of Israel and Judah (Jehoram and Jehoshaphat) are at war with the king of Moab. The deep and unresolvable conflict is symbolized by a terrible drought. The hope is to go from "no water" to "water," and the only way the kings know to do it is to go to war.

But Jehoshaphat wisely (or desperately) consults the prophet Elijah. The prophet does not want to be a simple tool in the agenda of a king and responds sarcastically, "Go to your father's prophets or to your mother's" (v. 13). Kings can always find pious people of position to justify what they have already decided to do. Even Hitler had his own "German Christians," bought pastors who sanctified his unholy business.

Elijah is no such lackey, no yes-man. Convinced of the king's sincerity, he finally consents to speak a word of the Lord, saying, "get me a musician" (v. 15). "And then, while the musician was playing, the power of the Lord came on him." The coming of water is predicted, and then fulfilled. The drought is over. The word of the Lord has broken through while the music plays. And it has come through the song of the prophet, not the declaration of the kings.

Wise leaders seek prophets. We do ourselves no favors when we curry only the affirmation of those who have only incentives to agree with us. Breakthrough is often sung through prophets who dwell in the realm of music when we have only been hearing and speaking prose.

Prayer: *Lord, grant me ears to hear the music of your prophetic voice underneath the droning of officials. Allow me to dwell in the world of the holy song and poem that transcends the prose of mere physical reality. Attune my heart to your divine frequency, and my lips to sing your praise, in the name of Jesus, men.*

John P. Chandler   131

2 KINGS 4

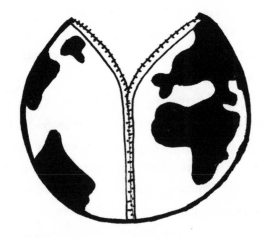

OPENING A CLOSED WORLD

"Elisha said to her, "What shall I do for you? Tell me, what do you have in your house?" – 2 Kings 4:2

Chapter 4 of Second Kings tells four successive stories of miracles brought about with the intervention of Elisha. The stories enhance Elisha's credibility by mimicking the stories of his powerful predecessor Elijah, and by foreshadowing similar works of Jesus Christ (feeding miracles, raising the dead).

We learn something about the **collaborative** nature of miracles in these stories. A poor woman offers the only jar in her house, and her neighbors help ... a rich woman builds a prophet's chamber ... servants gather herbs for stew ... a man sets his grain offering before the community. In all of these, a prophet speaks and God intervenes. But the recipe in each story includes the ingredients of human participation and contribution. We all play a part in our own miraculous solutions. God can do a lot with a little when God has all of it.

In these stories, the prophetic work of God is shown, like a jewel, to have at least four facets. A closed universe is opened by divine-human collaboration, and people move from:

- Poverty → Solvency (vv. 1-7)

- Death → Life (vv. 8-37)

- Rottenness → Nourishment (vv. 38-41)

- Hunger → Plenty (vv. 42-44)

The core work of a prophetic biblical leader is to speak and act to open up closed realities. Where kings fail, prophets don't. Communities are mobilized, the good news is spoken, and God moves so that people experience the "*shalom*" of having <u>enough</u>.

2 KINGS 5

TWO RESPONSES TO A PROPHETIC GIFT

*"Now I know that there is no God in all the earth except in
Israel; please accept a present from your servant."*
– 2 Kings 5:15

Praying the Kings

It is Elisha who brings the prophetic and transforming word in 2 Kings 5. The kings of Israel and Aram are such non-factors that they are not even named in the story. But the prophet can speak the word of God that changes everything. This chapter is about two possible and deeply contrasting responses to the divine gift offered by the prophet: Naaman, the Aramean commander, and Gehazi, the servant of Elisha.

Naaman	Gehazi
Outsider who is blessed (freed from leprosy)	Insider who is cursed (stricken with leprosy)
Arrogance →Servanthood	Servant role →Greedy opportunist
Commander →Worshipper	Assistant to prophet →Manipulator
Wealthy → Generosity	Humble →Deceptive
Offers "a present"	Tries to steal a present

Naaman accepts the gift of healing and makes an offering. Gehazi tries to take advantage of that same free gift and turn it into personal financial gain.

We, too, have options about how we respond to the free divine gifts of healing and God-given opportunities. Leaders who do not trust in their own wealth and power to transform will, like Naaman, receive from God a future they cannot manufacture for themselves. Those who deceptively mishandle God-given gifts will be brought low.

2 KINGS 6

SURROUNDED BY CHARIOTS OF FIRE

"His servant said, "Alas, master! What shall we do?" Elijah
replied, "Do not be afraid, for there are more with us than
there are with them." Then Elijah prayed, "O Lord, please
open his eyes that he may see." So the Lord opened the eyes
of the servant, and he saw; the mountains were full of horses
and chariots of fire all around Elisha." – 2 Kings 6:16-17

Elisha is a man of holy power, and as such has the ability to speak to the great reversals only possible through God. Through his speaking, iron ax heads float on water (vv. 1-7), and what were thought to be "superior" armies are sent home, humbled by a different kind of power (vv. 8-14, 18-23).

At the heart of Elisha's power is the sight and knowledge that, as a man of God, he operates within a camp that greatly outnumbers whatever human forces come up against him. Royal power in Israel didn't know this, and his own servant didn't perceive it. But Elisha is a person of power because he "sees" what others are "blind" to: that God's people are surrounded by a great cloud of witnesses, a holy army of angels, a heavenly host. He is free to offer generosity and hospitality instead of killing and war because of this power. He leads out of the strength of the invisible majority.

One day, Jesus Christ would echo this prophetic leadership, when he chose to go to the cross instead of overpowering what seemed to be foes that outnumbered him: *"Do you not think that I cannot appeal to my Father, and he will at once send me more than twelve legions of angels?"* (Matthew 26:53). He chose to give his life out of a position of strength, not weakness.

Those prophetic leaders who remember that we are surrounded by chariots of fire, a great cloud of witnesses, a communion of saints, can sing the words of the great hymn:

> *"This is my Father's World!*
> *O let me ne'er forget,*
> *That though the wrong seems oft so strong,*
> *God is the ruler yet."*

2 KINGS 7

"Why should I hope in the Lord any longer?" – **2 Kings 6:33**

"Those who wait for the Lord shall renew their strength, they shall mount up with wings like eagles, they shall run and not be weary, they shall walk and not faint." – **Isaiah 40:31**

Praying the Kings

Some days, the king gets to be Solomon. He speaks from the seat of power, babies are spared from death, even the poor get justice, and the king is lauded by all for his great wisdom and acknowledged as leader (1 Kings 3:16-28).

But other days, the king is Jehoram. There is famine in the land, he's wearing sackcloth, and he even plots with the poor in schemes to eat their own babies (2 Kings 6:24-30 – quite a symbol for "no future!"). What to do then?

It is difficult for kings to trust in power beyond the royal solutions. And Jehoram blames and rejects the prophet Elisha (and God) as the cause of famine in the land: *"This trouble is from the Lord!"* (6:33). There is more despair in doubting God's goodness than there is in denying God's power.

This story gives only a negative leader-example of failing to wait. But there is a more excellent way for the leader in the midst of famine. And that is to know that God is:

- ❧ Attentive to the cry of the poor (6:26-28);

- ❧ Present in the words of his prophets (7:1);

- ❧ Able to use even the outcast/lepers as part of the solution (7:3-10); and

- ❧ Willing *"to make windows in the sky"* (7:2) to provide for his people.

Again greater than ourselves.

John P. Chandler

2 KINGS 9

"Is it peace, Jehu?" He answered, "What peace can there be, so long as the many whoredoms and sorceries of your mother Jezebel continue?" – 2 Kings 9:22

Chapters 9-10 of Second Kings record seven acts of violence in a military coup. Four times, the question of peace ("*shalom*") is asked (vv. 17, 19, 22, 31); each time the response is met with violence or threat. Perhaps at times there must be violence if *shalom* is to be restored .... The interest in the story lies in the sovereign hand of God beneath the annals of history. The revolution is fomented by Elisha and the company of prophets (vv. 1ff); sometimes the prophetic people of God do this sort of thing! And story revolves around two concrete geographical sites: "*the property of Naboth*" (v. 21) and "*Jezreel*" (v. 30). Like Gettysburg, Pearl Harbor, and Selma, these places become deep symbols of much larger themes and truths:

> Regarding *Naboth*: this refers to King Ahab's trampling and stealing from "the powerless little guy" in 1 Kings 21;

> Regarding *Jezreel*: this is referred to years later in Hosea 1:5 and 2:22 as emblematic of the idolatry that destroyed *shalom*.

Beneath all of the realpolitik of coup and violence lies this one truth: "<u>God will not be mocked</u>." Real events happen in this world through real people. But underneath it all is the most real reality of all. And that is, that God is provident and sovereign over history. And God's regard for the way things should be in the world will finally prevail.

John P. Chandler   141

2 KINGS 12

TEMPLE REPAIR?

Jesus answered, "Destroy this temple, and in three days I will raise it up." The Jews then said, "This temple has been under construction for forty-six years, and you will raise it up in three days?" But he was speaking of the temple of his body. After he was raised from the dead, his disciples remembered that he had said this; and they believed the scripture and the word that Jesus had spoken." – John 2:19-22

It is years after the reign of wise king Solomon, and things have deteriorated quite badly. Jehoash (or "Joash") reigns 40 years, and even though he is described as a king who *did what was right in the sight of the Lord all his days*" (2 Kings 12:2), his legacy is mixed – mostly because it lacked the size, weightiness, and importance of Solomon's rule. He is a pale imitation of his wise predecessor. Jehoash's main contribution (2 Kings 12) was a reform of how offerings were collected and distributed for repairs of the temple. It is an accomplishment – but in the grand scheme of things, only a minor one. Things have rotted in Judah when a king's accomplishments are primarily administrative.

Perhaps the leadership takeaway is about the temple repair itself. Walter Brueggemann says, "*The temple symbolizes our best attempts to give our faith centrality and visibility in public life.*" Our buildings and programs symbolize the present and future hope that God's reign will one day govern all – "governance not yet established but fully promised." Temples are necessary – but not ultimate. They are mixed symbols. They embody the hopes of a people – but they always crumble and must give way to something larger than themselves.

Leaders understand this about the things they oversee. Our buildings and programs matter, but not finally. Finally, what matters is the reign of One who reigns over even kings. Jesus said, "*Destroy this temple, and in three days I will raise it up ... but he was speaking of the temple of his body*" (John 2:19). We are wise when we look to lead people in hoped-for things that far surpass their temporary embodiments. Build things, yes. Trust in those things that we build as ultimate? No. It is only the God to whom buildings and programs point who is worthy of our final trust and hope as leader and people.

John P. Chandler   143

2 KINGS 13

NO SUCCESSOR. NO SUCCESS

"Now when Elisha had fallen sick with the illness of which he was to die, King Joash of Israel went down to him and wept before him, saying, "My father, my father! The chariots of Israel and its horsemen!" – 2 Kings 13:12

From chapter 13-15, Second Kings covers about a century of history, mostly by listing the reigns of kings who were, in Walter Brueggemann's words, "*as inconsequential for Israel's faith and history as is James Buchanan in American history.*" One rises to power, lives with a mixed lukewarm rule, finally dies, and the cycle continues.

But now Elisha is set to die, and this is a big deal. Even King Joash acknowledges that Elisha is more powerful than his meager "*chariots and horsemen.*" Elisha has one more prophetic word, chiding the king for his half-heartedness, and then Elisha dies. Later we are told then even when the bones of a dead man touched the grave of Elisha, he sprung back to life. Elisha has more power dead than kings do alive!

But Elisha, who followed the equally-powerful Elijah, has no one to succeed him. The line of prophets ends. Israel is left to weak kings. The end is near for the nation, who spirals into slavery.

Without successors, there is no success. Every prophetic leader needs not only to do works of power in his or her own day, but to prepare someone to follow in his or her steps to do those same works. Elisha had a predecessor, but did not parlay this into having a successor. Jesus worked unique miracles, yes. But his most significant work might be found in making disciples of twelve around him, who became the church. Through his successors, the world is a very different place.

Prayer: *O Lord, give me eyes to tap into the power of prophets in my own day. And grant me wisdom to identify the one(s) who will come after me to carry on the holy work that you have given to us. I ask that you make me obedient to "make disciples of all nations," just as Jesus did and commanded us to do. In his name, Amen.*

John P. Chandler

2 KINGS 16

BEYOND APPEASEMENT

"(Ahaz) did not do what was right in the sight of the Lord his God, as his ancestor David had done, but he walked in the way of the kings of Israel." – 2 Kings 16:2-3

King Ahaz of 2 Kings 16 is the archetype of an evil leader. According to Amos, Isaiah, and the Chronicler, "*he did not do what was right in the sight of the Lord his God, as his ancestor David had done, but he walked in the way of the kings of Israel*" (vv. 2f). Biblical leaders are not graded on the curve of their "control group" of peers, but on a different standard.

There are three primary factors describing the failure of Ahaz as a king and leader:

1. He reinstituted Canaanite religious practices, including child sacrifice (v. 3) – is there any more graphic symbol of giving away the future?!

2. He appeased an aggressive tyrant, the king of Assyria, paying him a bribe (vv. 7-9) ironically financed from the "*house of the Lord.*" The king of Assyria was glad to be paid for what he intended to do anyway.

3. He dismantled the temple (vv. 17f), undoing the glory of Solomon, to pay for his "*present*" to the opposing king.

The anti-leader thus:

෨ Sacrifices the future (children);

෨ Bribes rather than confronts tyrants;

෨ Dismantles sacred space and tradition.

Sometimes the biblical text gives us leaders to emulate. Other times, such as with Ahaz, it gives clear pictures of warning and thus teaches us to grow a spine and flee in the opposite direction.

John P. Chandler   147

2 KINGS 17

THE PROPHETIC OUTSIDER

"Then the king of Assyria commanded, "Send there one of the priests whom you carried away from there; let him go and live there, and teach them the law of the god of the land." – 2 Kings 17:27

Praying the Kings

Second Kings 17 describes the final spiraling demise of Israel as the nation is taken off into Exile by Assyria. Decidedly, it is not Assyria but Israel who is to blame for the undoing of Solomon's glory. The reversal of Exodus liberation has happened because of Israel's insistent refusal to be true to its own covenant identity. The verbs indicting Israel pile up in verses 7-18: "*worshiped other gods ... walked in the customs of the nations ... secretly did things that were not right ... did wicked things ... served idols ... would not listen* (the core demand of Israel's faith!) *... despised his statutes ... went after false idols ... rejected commandments*"...the list goes on and on.

In a great irony, the king of Assyria brings in an occupying army. Covenant *Israel* no longer exists; it is renamed *Samaria* to mark its unalterable contamination. But God is not mocked, and as the new settlers ignorantly do not fear Yahweh, they are killed by lions. Alarmed, the king of Assyria gives the instruction for an exiled Israelite priest to go back into Israel and teach the covenant law!

We are fast trending toward a day when the United States receives more Christian missionaries than it sends. Perhaps this should remind us that when we have become blind to our own compromise and syncretism, a prophetic outsider can ironically speak clarity and truth to call us back to our true identity. A great leader is willing to look outside of her/his own closed system for a fresh and prophetic voice, for someone willing who may be living closer to our identity than we are. May we have the courage to ask for that, and to listen.

John P. Chandler   149

2 KINGS 18

"Moreover, is it without the Lord that I have come up against this place to destroy it? The Lord said to me, "Go up against this land and destroy it." – 2 Kings 18:25

The final section of the books of Kings (2 Kings 18-25) offers seven portraits of leaders of Judah as the nation spirals toward exile. Hezekiah's featured story (chapters 18-20) is mostly one of a leader who *"trusted in the Lord the God of Israel"* (v. 5) and thus experienced prosperity and liberation.

But trust is always tested and tempted, and Hezekiah is not exempt. The leaders of Assyria come to challenge Hezekiah's trust in God. Demanding surrender, they make four arguments: a). your allies are weak; b). your king is compromised; c). your armies are weak; and finally, most importantly, d). we have been sent by God to do this work (v. 25). Who can argue with that?

Wise leaders, though, do not automatically assume that everyone who says "God sent me!" is actually sent by God. The serpent in Genesis 3 claims to be in league with God. The devil, in tempting Jesus, (Matthew 4, Luke 4) claims to speak for God. And the Assyrians who claim to be sent by God are merely using God-language to intimidate. And Hezekiah ultimately (rightly) resists those claims.

When someone comes to me and wants to direct my decisions based on "What God told me to tell you to do," my learned response is to say, "When God tells me to do it, then I will do it." The best Christian leaders "test the spirits," discerning the claims of those who would speak for God against what the Bible and community of faith say. Not everyone who claims to speak for God is actually speaking for God.

2 KINGS 20

FOURTH QUARTER SELL-OUT

"Then Hezekiah said to Isaiah, "The word you have spoken is good." For he thought, "Why not, if there will be peace and security in my days?" – 2 Kings 20:19

Praying the Kings

King Hezekiah has been a great leader, a "*wonderful counselor and Prince of Peace*" (Isaiah 9:6) for Judah. But now is his time to die. He prays, begs, cries, cajoles, and bargains with God. (Prayer can do that: it can ask, seek, and knock.) And God responds to prayer by healing him, adding fifteen years to his life! Yes, God can turn back time and reverse sickness when we pray.

But what Hezekiah does with that extra 15 years is a travesty. In ill-advised hospitality, he "*plays footsie with a worldly power for a moment of peace*" (Walter Brueggemann). He makes an alliance with Babylonians who will eventually turn on Judah and lead them into Exile. When the prophet Isaiah confronts King Hezekiah about this, the king's response is stunning: as long as things are secure while I am alive, "*security in my days,*" he says, who cares what happens in the future?

Like king Solomon before him, Hezekiah played a great game until fumbling badly late in the fourth quarter. He undid a history of wisdom with late-game folly. In selling out by appeasing God-mockers, he undermined the long-term welfare of his people, and his own legacy. He was followed by Manasseh, the most wicked king Judah had seen in a century, and the nation quickly spiraled south.

We haven't led well until we have finished well.

Prayer: *God, please help me to walk with you to the end, to bring to completion the good work you began in me and through me. Help me not to undermine a legacy of prayerful trust through late acts of unfaith. Give me the grace to sprint through the finish line of your call for my life and leadership. In the name of Jesus, who ran the race and finished the course and won the prize, Amen."*

---

2 KINGS 21

LESSONS FROM THE
WORST KING OF JUDAH

"I will wipe Jerusalem as one wipes a dish." – 2 Kings 21:13

Sandwiched between two devout kings, Hezekiah and Josiah, king Manasseh is widely regarded as the worst king in Judah's history – and the cause of her Exile in Babylon later. His laundry list of despicable acts culminates in the summary that he *"misled them to do more evil than the nations"* (v. 9).

God's verdict on this evil reign is captured in three metaphors. God will:

1. do something in Jerusalem that causes *"the ears of everyone who hears of it to tingle";*

2. stretch out a *"measuring line"* or plumb line over the nation; and

3. *"wipe Jerusalem as one wipes a dish."*

And yet, Manasseh reigns fifty-five years (v. 1) and is given a peaceful burial (v. 18). What gives?

The cleanest lesson is that while compromise can keep you on the throne for a long time, God is neither fooled by human successes nor by longevity. There is a different plumb line for the devout leader.

And just because you've been in an official role of leadership for a long time ... that doesn't automatically make you a leader.

2 KINGS 22

THE HEART OF A LEADER

"When the king heard the words of the book of the law, he tore his clothes." – 2 Kings 22:11

The nation of Judah is spiraling toward an unalterable Exile because of its dishonesty. Yet significant mention is given to faithful (and young) king Josiah. From ages eight to eighteen, he "*did what was right in the sight of the Lord.*" This grounding prepared him for proper leadership later. It's never too early to form a future leader!

During temple repairs, a book of the Torah (Deuteronomy) is found. It is so foreign that the discoverer likely has no clue as to what it is, or how important it is. But Josiah does. "*His heart was penitent*" and he "*humbled*" himself and "*wept*" before God. Based on the alarming uncovering of a gap between public policy and God's expectations, Josiah then begins a series of public reforms. It turns out to be too-little-too-late for the nation, but the king is commended as a model of responsiveness to God.

Public leadership begins in private formation and personal penitence. Repentance of the leader (for himself/herself and on behalf of the people s/he leads) is the first step toward public reform. Leadership always begins with turning of the heart of the leader.

Prayer: *Create in me a clean heart, O God, and renew a right spirit within me. Cast me not away from your presence and take not your Holy Spirit from me. Restore unto me the joy of salvation, and sustain in me a willing spirit. Then I will teach transgressors their ways, and sinners will return to you (Psalm 51:10-12). In the name of Jesus, Amen.*

---

2 KINGS 23

PERSONAL
REPENTANCE

PUBLIC
REFORM

*"The king commanded all the people, "Keep the Passover
to the Lord your God as prescribed in this book of the
covenant." No such Passover had been kept since the days
of the judges who judged Israel ... but in the eighteenth
year of King Josiah, this Passover was kept to the Lord in
Jerusalem." –* **2 Kings 23:21-23**

Young King Josiah has responded to the rediscovery of a life-guiding Torah amidst the rubble of a temple in disrepair. The people of Judah have wondered so far from God that they "don't know what they don't know." But Josiah sees how far Judah has wandered from the covenant law, and he is cut to the heart.

But personal repentance without public reform is empty. As the New Testament would later say, "*Faith, by itself, if it has no works, is dead*" (James 2:17). King Josiah implements a radical and widespread program of religious reforms that clarifies public and political loyalties. The capstone act of this is to reinstitute a long-neglected Passover celebration.

Great leaders always recover powerful symbols of public liberation which name and solidify the best of what people are to become. Josiah remembered the Passover. An American political leader might reinstitute the sweeping vision captured in *America the Beautiful*. Jesus of Nazareth told his followers to remember him in the breaking of the bread and sharing of the cup, a reform of life together that continues to change the world.

Passover, anthem, cup ... leaders know that the rituals of reform matter.

John P. Chandler   159

1 CHRONICLES 13

CONSULTING WITH COMMANDERS

"David consulted with the commanders of the thousands and of the hundreds, with every leader. David said to the whole assembly of Israel, "If it seems good to you, and if it is the will of the Lord our God ..." – 1 Chronicles 13:1-2

The book of Chronicles tells the story of David from a different "flashback" perspective than that of the books of Samuel and Kings. In Chronicles, David is great, first and most, because he leads Israel in *worship*. It's not his military prowess or personal shortcomings that interest the writer; it is his faithfulness to God and ability to lead a nation into the same faithfulness.

This holiness inspires stories of incredible devotion from others. Chapters 11-12 tell tales of "*the Three*" and "*the Thirty*" who go to heroic lengths in the service of their leader. David is clearly able to muster and deploy the strengths of many. How does he do this?

One secret lies in his artistic balance of taking input and making royal decisions. 13:1 says that David "*consulted with the commanders*" about the decision to bring the Ark of God into Jerusalem. He also spoke to the nation saying, "*if it seems good to you <u>and</u> if it is the will of the Lord our God.*" This both includes their input, and puts it in the larger framework of the leader's unique roles:

- ☙ To discern divine guidance;

- ☙ To gather consensus; and

- ☙ To voice a decision.

David was great because he figured out how to give leaders and the nation a say in the matter while retaining the royal right to make a decision. It took several (failed) attempts to bring the ark into Jerusalem, but David was finally able to do it. His ability to withstand failed attempts was based in the reality that he gained the ownership and loyalty of his people as part of leading.

Prayer: *Lord, give me today the ability to listen to your voice through the wisdom of others, and the art of depending not entirely and finally on their voices alone. Help me to lead in that good space between being a weathervane of windy public opinion and a bully. Base my greatness as a leader in my closeness to you and with those who lead with me. In the name of Jesus who did this, Amen.*

John P. Chandler   161

1 CHRONICLES 15

GATE KEEPERS

"David also commanded ... gatekeepers"
– 1 Chronicles 15:16-23

In the book of Chronicles, king David is first and most a worship leader and not a military general or personal hero. His greatest triumph is not victory over the Philistines or capture of Jerusalem, but the recovery of the Ark of the Covenant and bringing it in as the center of the city and kingdom he will rule as a priest-king. He wears an ephod, not a crown.

Part of his leadership is to appoint three chief psalmists and fourteen secondary worship leaders from the clan of the Levites to supervise the all-important importing of the ark into Jerusalem. The three psalmists (Heman, Asaph, and Ethan) are later found in the book of psalms; their compositions become part of the worship-book of the people of God.

These three are called, "*gatekeepers*" (vv. 18, 23). A gatekeeper is one who stands as the guardian of a threshold. As musicians, these leaders stood in the liminal place between holy/unholy, clean/unclean, righteous/unrighteous. They helped people keep faith and prevented the Lord from "*bursting out*" (v. 13) because of improper inattention toward God.

A great leader, like David, will recognize the primary important of music and arts in leading a whole people toward a righteous vision. Great music and great art is an invaluable part of mobilizing the people toward the vision of a holy and righteous city.

Prayer: *Lord, grant me vision to see and hear through the eyes and ears of great artists today. Let them inspire our people to heights of faithfulness to a righteous vision of a holy city. Thank you for people who see and hear the world so differently and so beautifully. Amen.*

---

1 CHRONICLES 17

WHAT 'EASE' CAN DO
TO A LEADER

"Now when David settled in his house, David said to the prophet Nathan, "I am living in a house of cedar, but the ark of the covenant of the Lord is under a tent." Nathan said to David, "Do all that you have in mind, for God is with you."
– 1 Chronicles 17:1-2

Much is made of David as the greatest leader in the history of Israel. God promised a dynasty in his name forever, and even Babylonian Exile couldn't destroy that. Christians acknowledged Jesus as "*son of David*" because he is in line with this great leader.

First Chronicles 17 gives a glimpse into what made David great. Because of his military accomplishments, David sired a great household and became very wealthy. Living in a "*house of cedar*" indicated powerful, wealthy, and blessed status. But David's prosperity did not insulate him from a sense of call and generosity. And even though the actual building of the temple eventually fell to his son, Solomon, rather than to him, David's heart and generosity were indispensible for that to occur.

A great leader is one who, when s/he lives in a "*house of cedar*," is not insulated from calling and generosity. "Ease" does not pacify or dull such leaders. They do not settle for making the world a better place for themselves, but use their platform for the healing and repair of creation – in this way mimicking God, who in creation ceased to be everything so that we could become something.

Prayer: *God, we are truly wealthy and truly blessed. Guard us from laziness and fill us with a sense of the responsibility that comes with our prosperity. You have given us a platform from which to lead; now stoke our passion and compassion, so that we may do much with what we have been given. Keep us from arrogance, and fill us with prayerfulness, generosity, and humility that you would use us in your great work in the world. In the name of Jesus our leader we pray, Amen.*

John P. Chandler

1 CHRONICLES 21

HOLY DISOBEDIENCE

"But he did not include Levi and Benjamin in the numbering,
for the king's command was abhorrent to Joab."
– 1 Chronicles 21:6

According to the book of Chronicles, the great sin of King David was not his adulterous affair with Bathsheba (not even mentioned!), but his orders for a census. David wanted a census in order to tax people, to assess the labor pool, and for the military draft. We are not told directly why this was counted as a vile sin in Israel; some have suggested that it is a reflection of pride or insecurity, an act of distrusting God. Whatever the reason, David is tempted to order one, and (against strong advice) he carries it out. The rest of the chapter mostly deals with the painful consequences of David's disobedience to God.

But in verses 3-6, another kind of disobedience is worth noting. Joab, David's right hand military man, is charged with carrying out the census. It is *"abhorrent"* to him – meaning that, beyond personal dislike, it is a personal, ritual and spiritual sin for him to do so. What is Joab to do when the king orders him to violate his conscience?

What he does is obey – to a point. By not numbering the set-apart tribes of the Levites and Benjamites, Joab obeys direct orders, but is also selectively disobedient at the point of conscience. It's not out of simple personal preference; it's that Joab ultimately fears his divine master more than his human master.

An elder leader, Reggie McDonough, once gave me great counsel. "The purpose of leadership," he said, "is to make exceptions to policy." Policy is a serious matter in that its protocols represent a kind of community consensus necessary for rule of law and civil society. But just as Nuremburg taught us that "following orders" was no excuse for carrying out genocide, leaders like Joab must sometimes, in fear and trembling, exercise holy disobedience. Policy matters. But leaders sometimes make exceptions to policy.

After all, Jesus was ultimately executed by Rome as a law-breaker.

John P. Chandler   167

1 CHRONICLES 27

LISTENING to COUNSELORS

"Jonathan, David's uncle, was a counselor, being a man of understanding and a scribe ... Ahithophel was the king's counselor, and Hushai the Archite was the king's friend."
– 1 Chronicles 27:32-33

From I Chronicles 23-27, much is made of David's organization of the worship life of Israel. His military savvy, for instance, takes a back seat to this primary role of leading his people to the proper worship of God.

At the end of this long section, the writer turns to David's civic leadership. It describes his organization of society according to military (vv. 1-15), tribal (vv. 16-24), and business (vv. 25-31) leaders. Finally, there is a listing of six of David's advisors/counselors (vv. 32-34).

Interestingly, what passes without comment in this list is David's mixed legacy of listening to his wise counselors. Ahithophel gives un-followed advice and commits suicide (2 Samuel 17:23). Hushai has to mask his advice with un-truth in order to have it followed 2 Sam.15:37). Abiathar sides with the (wrong) rival to Solomon's throne (I Kings 1:7). And the one time Joab gave David advice (I Chronicles 21:3), David ignores it and is thumped by God! Why, then, this elevated list of David's wise counselors, in light of their very-spotty track record?

The leadership lesson is that we should both have a team of wise advisors around us ... and should be circumspect about listening to them. Being an official counselor doesn't automatically make anyone wise. But neither is "going it alone" advised for any ruler. Wise leadership comes in spirited conversation between "those in charge" and those who counsel them. Every leader should have a "personal board of directors" around him/her, giving insight and perspectives on character and decisions. Who is on yours?

Prayer: *God, give me the wisdom to put wise people around me today. Give me discernment to listen well. And grant me the courage to act on my convictions in light of the advice I receive, neither controlled nor unaffected by it. Help me to lead communities in community. In the name of Jesus, who traveled with disciples, Amen.*

John P. Chandler

1 CHRONICLES 29

*"I know, my God, that you search the heart, and take
pleasure in uprightness; in the uprightness of my heart I have
freely offered all these things, and now I have seen your
people, who are present here, offering freely and joyously
to you." – 1 Chronicles 29:17*

The last chapter of the book of First Chronicles records the final, "legacy" speech of King David. David is regarded as the one who casts the longest shadow of greatness in Israel. Just as Moses administered the Law of God, David administered the liturgy of God for the people. It is now time for him to die and to pass along his rule to his successor. How does he do so?

Two things mark the transition in the farewell speech. One, David acknowledges that God's kingship undergirds his own human kingship:

> *"Yours, O Lord, are the greatness, the power, the glory, the victory, and the majesty; for all that is in the heavens and on the earth is yours; Yours is the kingdom, O Lord, and you are exalted as head over all"*
> *(29:11).*

Christians recognize the parallel of these words with those that close the Lord's Prayer that Jesus taught his disciples (Matthew 6:13).

Second, David's final act as a leader in blessing his successor and people was to lead by being the lead giver. His legacy was his own personal generosity (v. 3) and leading leaders (v. 6) and people (vv. 9, 21) to give freely, cheerfully, and abundantly to God and the house of God.

At the end of our lives, we will be most remembered for what we have *given* and led others to give. Legacy is measured by generosity, not accumulation. Leaders who give well bless those who come behind them, and mimic the divine Source who is the fountain of everything we have.

John P. Chandler   171

2 CHRONICLES 2

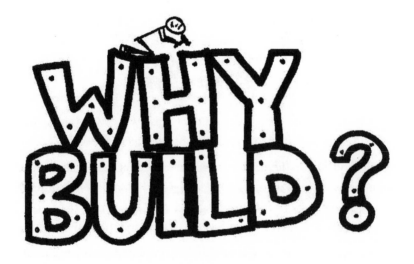

"Who am I to build a house for God, except as a place to make offerings for him?" – **2 Chronicles 2:6**

The second book of Chronicles begins with the story of Solomon. Nine chapters detail the essence of the wisest and wealthiest king who ever ruled Israel. Six of those nine chapters describe Solomon's building of the temple. Temple-building embodies Solomon's God-given wisdom and was the highest expression of his rule.

The Bible goes into great detail about the construction and furnishing of this temple. It is fantastically opulent, a testimony to the greatness of God. Solomon, however, makes the foundational statement about this building: *"Who am I to build a house for him, except as a place to make offerings before him?"* (v. 6). The building is thus a means to an end: it is a place to make offerings, worship, and sacrifice. Symbolically reinforcing this idea, 3:1 tells us that the location of the temple was on a spot where king David had made a significant sacrifice.

Leaders often build buildings. Sometimes these are monuments to the ego and power of the leader. But a great leader will only build when that building becomes a furtherance in helping people to give, worship, and sacrifice. We need a temple because no one gets called to love the poor simply by walking alone through the woods. But when a community comes together in a temple to give thanks to the Great Giver, we find together the call to help the needy and to be people of generosity and humility.

Why build, and what to build? Build when the building helps others to become people of sacrifice.

2 CHRONICLES 5-6

TALKING TO GOD. TALKING TO PEOPLE

"I have built you an exalted house, a place for you to reside in forever." Then the king turned around and blessed all the assembly of Israel, while all the assembly of Israel stood."
– 2 Chronicles 6:2-3

King Solomon has completed the pinnacle work of his father David, and the temple is ready for the people of God to occupy. Celebrated during the feast of Succoth and its celebration of the giving of the Law, the dedication thus connects the faith and heart of David (temple) with the Law and guidance of Moses (Law). As the New Testament would later put it, *"faith without works is dead"* (James 2:26).

Solomon and the elders lead the ark of the covenant into the temple, for without the presence of God symbolized in the ark, the temple is simply another impressive building and not a holy place. The musicians carry out their "duty" to *"make themselves heard in unison in praise and thanksgiving to the Lord"* (5:13), fulfilling their prophetic role. Music, as it turns out, is not a frill for worship, but is an indispensible way of mediating the presence of God.

Finally, feeling God's presence so intensely that it was like a *"cloud"* (vv. 13f), Solomon speaks. How he speaks is critical: he turns first to address God (v. 1) about the work of the temple, and then *"turned around and blessed all the assembly."*

Leaders can learn something simple but profound by watching this pattern. That is, one turns to speak to God before turning to speak to the people. It works so much better that way than the alternatives!

Prayer: *Lord, let me early in the morning find myself in your presence, speaking to you, listening to you. And let this holy conversation form the foundation of every encounter that I have today with the people to whom you have entrusted me to lead and care for. In the name of Jesus our Lord, Amen.*

---

2 CHRONICLES 15

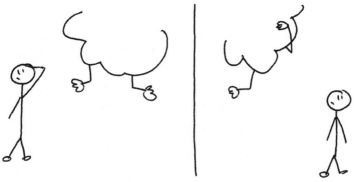

SEEKING AND BEING SOUGHT

"For a long time Israel was without the true God, and without a teaching priest and without law; but when in their distress they turned to the Lord, the God of Israel, and sought him, he was found by them ... For the eyes of the Lord range throughout the entire earth, to strengthen those whose heart is true to him." – 2 Chronicles 15:3-4, 9

For long stretches, Israel lacked dynamic point leadership. Much of 2 Chronicles describes times between the peak international power of David and Solomon, and the great reforms of Hezekiah and Josiah. Instead, we have chapter after chapter of the likes of kings Abijah, Baasha, and here, Asa. Even the prophet Azariah of chapter 15 pales in comparison to later prophets like Isaiah and Jeremiah. Why so much space for so many shrug-worthy leaders?

First, let it be said that the reigns of prophet Azariah and king Asa were not without merit. They told the truth and enacted reforms. Just because they weren't famous leaders doesn't mean they were worthless leaders.

One angle for the list of listless leaders is that they highlight the need of the people to turn to God as their leader. No king or prophet can do for people what God can do. And the book of Chronicles is a sustained attempt to get people to turn to God as leader. *"If my people, who are called by my name, humble themselves, pray, seek my face, and turn from their wicked ways, then I will hear from heaven, and will forgive their sin and heal their land"* (2 Chronicles 7:14). This is the core message. The prophet is constantly imploring people to seek God as leader.

But the best news of chapter 15 is not that people can seek God; it's that God is seeking *them*. Indeed, *"the eyes of the Lord range throughout the entire earth."* God is actively looking for earnest people with a goal to *"strengthen those whose heart is true to him."*

Search as we may for dynamic leaders, and hopeful as it is that we might find God if we seek, the best news we will ever hear is that God is searching for us. We can seek – but, better yet, we are being sought.

John P. Chandler

2 CHRONICLES 21-23

"He departed with no one's regret." – 2 Chronicles 21:20

Like many sections of the book, 2 Chronicles 21-23 describes the non-descript reigns of wicked kings and one queen: kings Jehoram and Ahaziah, and queen Athaliah. Never heard of them? There's a reason for that; they were terrible rulers.

Some have speculated that the negative evaluation of queen Athaliah (Judah's one and only queen ruler) is yet another example of the virulent sexism of the Bible. But you would have to make that case on other grounds than the text itself. She is rejected as a ruler because, like her infamous mother Jezebel, she does not worship the God of Israel. Athaliah is not even found in the temple on a Sabbath when a religious coup takes place. No wonder her calls of "*Treason!*" are ignored and she meets an ignoble death.

Perhaps the most concise summary of the negative assessment of these unholy rulers is the one that describes the demise of Jehoram:

> ❧ In his own person: "*the Lord struck him in his bowels with an incurable disease ... and he died in great agony*" (21:18f);
>
> ❧ In society: "*His people made no fire in his honor, like the fires made for his ancestors*" (v. 19);
>
> ❧ In legacy: "*He departed with no one's regret*" (v. 20).

What a terrible coda for a ruler – or for a life!

Poor, impious leadership can bear its costs on the body of the leader, on their reputation, and on history's assessment of their stewardship of rule.

John P. Chandler 179

2 CHRONICLES 24

"All the leaders and all the people rejoiced and brought their tax and dropped it into the chest until it was full."
– 2 Chronicles 24:10

King Joash's story is like many others in the book of Chronicles. He had a faithful beginning and ruled well while under the mentorship of priest Jehoiada. After the death of his advisor, though, he slipped into the same apostasy that had bedeviled his grandmother (queen Athaliah), and was assassinated in disgrace (vv. 23-26).

The example of Joash's successful leadership has to do with collecting taxes to repair the neglected temple. Initially, his strategy was to send the priests out to the people. *"See that you act quickly,"* he said to them. *"But the Levites did not act quickly"* (v. 6) and the project languished. It is a surprising inertia, considering that the Temple was the domain of the Levites – classic bureaucracy and mission-drift.

Joash's solution is to appeal to the people throughout Jerusalem and stoke the fires of their vision of a restored temple. He cites Moses and the Torah, and *"A proclamation was made throughout Judah and Jerusalem to bring in for the Lord the tax"* (v. 9). The leaders then modeled faithfulness by bringing their offerings first. And lo and behold, the people not only followed suit, but *"rejoiced"* (v. 10) in doing so. Thus instituted the practice of people bringing their offering to the temple rather than officials hunting them down to collect it.

Good leaders, through vision, help people take ownership for the solutions to their society's problems. We can command all we want. But when we spark the best hopes that reside in people, they will come with the collective solutions to collective problems, and do it with enthusiasm.

2 CHRONICLES 25

NOT LISTENING TO WARNINGS

"But Amaziah would not listen – it was God's doing, in order to hand them over, because they had sought the gods of Edom." – 2 Chronicles 25:20

Amaziah is one in a series of kings (Joash, Uzziah, 2 Chronicles 24-26) who had good beginnings followed by bad endings. Like their prototype, king Solomon, their royal legacies were tainted by finishing poorly, and they are given poor grades by the biblical writers.

The early clue to Amaziah's eventual downfall is in v. 2: "*He did what was right in the sight of the Lord, yet not with a true heart.*" He did not lead with a "*single eye*" (Matthew 6:22-24) and was thus finally able to be led astray.

Amaziah's lead distraction was financial. He worried about the cost of hiring a mercenary army (v. 9) and could not bring himself to destroy the booty/foreign gods of captured enemies (vv. 14f). Those golden gods were his downfall. He worshiped them, thus rejecting the God who gave him victory in the first place.

Twice, king Amaziah is sent nameless prophets (vv. 7, 15). He refuses to listen and threatens to kill the prophet. However, he learns the hard way that while you can kill the messenger, you can't kill the message when it is from God. And so Amaziah marches into a foolish battle, is overthrown, all booty is carried off, and he dies in disgrace.

Leaders best be attuned to the nameless "prophets" sent our way to advise us to faithfulness. Not everyone who counsels us does so as a mouthpiece of God. But if we become so distracted or divided that we are unable to listen to the warnings of prophets (even non-famous ones), we will do ourselves in.

Prayer: *God, grant me this day a wise and discerning ear to listen to the right advice and wise counsel of the prophets you have put in my path. Keep my heart pure, eye single, and ears open, so that I may lead in response to your guidance. In the name of Jesus, Amen.*

John P. Chandler 183

2 CHRONICLES 26

FINISHING WELL

"And his fame spread far, for he was marvelously helped until he became strong. But when he had become strong he grew proud, to his destruction." – 2 Chronicles 26:15-16

King Uzziah was the last in a series of kings who received mixed reviews from the Chronicles of Judah. He is most well-known from his mention as the ruler when the prophet Isaiah had his famous vision of commissioning from God (Isaiah 6).

Uzziah gets a thumbs up for many reasons. His fifty-two year rule began well because he attached himself to a mentor (v. 5, Zechariah) who *"instructed him"* so that he would *"prosper."* The king also built cities, won military victories, oversaw the invention of new weapons (the catapult, vv. 14f), and *"loved the soil"* (v. 10). No wonder his *"fame spread far."*

But like other kings before him, his strength led to arrogance. The same sun that melts the butter hardens the clay. Like king Saul years earlier (1 Samuel 13), Uzziah overstepped his limits and attempted to make offerings that only priests were allowed to make. Just because you are king does not mean you can approach God casually. Uzziah is struck with disfiguring leprosy, pronounced unclean (by the priests, ironically!), and ends his reign in isolation, with his son Jotham having to serve as the functional governor.

Herein lies a lesson for every leader, made repeatedly in the Bible:

&ir; To begin well is good.

&ir; To continue well is better.

&ir; To finish well is best of all!

Prayer: *God, grant me the grace to run the race with perseverance and without fainting near the end. Let me finish well, fight the good fight to the last round, and like my savior Jesus, help me to serve all the way to the point of my death, and to die well. Amen."*

John P. Chandler   185

2 CHRONICLES 28

DEFEAT WITHOUT DISGRACE

*"Because the Lord, the God of your ancestors, was angry
with Judah, he gave them into your hand, but you have killed
them in a rage that has reached up to heaven."*
– 2 Chronicles 28:9

The Chronicler's story of king Ahaz is one of an unrepentantly wicked king whose principle sin was a vigorous and foolish willingness to entangle a set-apart Judah with unreliable and oppressive foreign alliances. Rather than trusting the Lord, Ahaz time and again leaned on pagan kings and was stained by their bad worship and fickleness. He didn't learn the old southern proverb, "If a dog will bite you once, he'll bite you twice!"

Embedded within this story is an incident of the northern kingdom of Israel taking captive their kin in southern Judah. As they were bringing their humiliated captives and all the booty back north, they are interrupted by a prophet Obed, who stops them in their tracks. Obed tells the victors that it was God's doing that they won the victory, but their *"rage"* over their defeated opponents stank to high heaven – especially since the captors and captives were kin. In short, this was a family feud, and you can't destroy family members when you are fighting with them. Win yes; shame, no. Victory, yes; rage, no.

To their credit, the northern kingdom repented, treated their captives kindly, fed and anointed them, and released them to freedom. Perhaps Jesus had this story in mind when he later spoke of the Good Samaritan (from the north) who, unlike the priest and Levite (from the south) rightly showed compassion to the down and out.

Leaders will sometimes get in showdowns and be forced into win-lose situations. This story shows that wise leaders, when possible, may defeat their opponents, but do well not to disgrace them.

2 CHRONICLES 30

LEADING PEOPLE FROM
WHERE THEY ARE

"Hezekiah prayed ... "The good Lord pardon all who set their hearts to seek God, the Lord the God of their ancestors, even though not in accordance with the sanctuary's rules of cleanness." The Lord heard Hezekiah, and healed the people." – 2 Chronicles 30:18-20

No one can accuse the Chronicler of not caring about high standards and "the rules." Much of the book evaluates the effectiveness of its royal leaders based on whether or not they adhered to proper worship and the Torah – and even their vigor to oppose laxity in these matters. Written as a retrospective after the Babylonian Exile of 586, Chronicles interprets the plight of Judah to their playing loosey-goosey with God's high expectations.

This makes the prayer of king Hezekiah remarkable. He has issued a call to gather the entire nation (including wayward Israel) to the temple for a Passover celebration. Many who heed the call have backslidden far from God and are ritually impure; they *"had not cleansed themselves"* and thus *"they ate the Passover otherwise than as prescribed"* (v. 18). Yet rather than turning them away, Hezekiah prayed for and included them in the festival.

This is a remarkable theological innovation. It puts internal intent ahead of external conformity and purity. It would later be developed by the prophet Micah (6:8) and by Jesus (Matthew 23:23).

Sometimes leaders have to hold the banner high and watch in pain while incapable people fail to jump high enough to reach it. Other times, like Hezekiah, leaders are wise to honor the intent of not-yet-capable responders and work with their intent to change even before the fruit of change is visible. Only leaders of prayer and wisdom can know when and how to do this.

John P. Chandler

2 CHRONICLES 33

THE POSSIBILITY OF A TURN AROUND

"While he was in distress he entreated the favor of the Lord his God and humbled himself greatly before the God of his ancestors. He prayed to him, and God received his entreaty, heard his plea, and restored him to Jerusalem and to his kingdom. Then Manasseh knew that the Lord was indeed God." – 2 Chronicles 33:12-13

Using different sources, the book of Chronicles tells many of the same stories as the book of Kings, but with different interpretations and points of emphasis. An example of this is with king Manasseh. Both Kings and Chronicles agree that this ruler of fifty-five years (longest in Judah's history) had a terrible beginning, actively undoing the religious reforms of his father and predecessor, the great king Hezekiah (2 Chronicle 29-32). The book of Kings ends with this terrible assessment of Manasseh's life.

But Chronicles tells his story differently. Here, Manasseh's unfaithfulness led to the Assyrians conquering Judah and leading the king away to captivity in manacles and fetters. But verse 12 shows a king in distress humbly turning to God in prayer. And because of this humility and entreaty, God restores the fallen king (v. 13). Manasseh went on to rebuild Jerusalem (v. 14) and enact positive religious reforms (vv. 15-16).

Why does Chronicles tell the story of Manasseh so differently? Because it is very important in the Bible to portray that the vilest sinner who turns toward God can be restored. Consider Paul in the New Testament – a self-described "*vile*" person who turned through "*grace*" (1 Corinthians 15:9f). As 1 John 1:9 puts it, "*If we confess our sins, he who is faithful and just will forgive us our sins and cleanse us from all unrighteousness.*"

This Old Testament story of grace to Manasseh reminds us that leaders must never write off anyone as irrevocably beyond the pale of grace. We have to make decisive evaluations of people sometimes. But wise leaders never discount the possibility of turnaround, and look for how even a fallen person might, through humility and prayer, yet make a contribution toward the restoration of the Kingdom.

John P. Chandler

2 CHRONICLES 34

EMOTION AND COMPULSION

"Because you ... have torn your clothes and wept before me, I also have heard you, says the Lord." – 2 Chronicles 34:27

Anointed as king at age eight, Josiah began to seek God *"while he was still a boy"* (v. 3) and purge the land of idols as soon as he was an adult leader. He began his rule as a vassal of *"the people of the land"* who made him king (33:25), but soon came into his own as the last great reformer king of Judah. His work was too little, too late to save the nation from Babylonian exile, but he did all that any leader could do.

While repairing the temple, Josiah's workers discover *"the book of the law"* (v. 14), probably Deuteronomy. His response to this discovery of the plumb line of just how far his people (including his own father, king Manasseh) had strayed was noteworthy. He was:

1. Emotional – the king famously *"tore his clothes"* (v. 19). Clearly his *"heart was penitent"* and *"humbled"* and he *"wept"* openly (v. 27). It was a demonstrative personal and public reaction.

2. Directive – the king *"made all who were in Israel worship the Lord their God"* (vv. 32f). He compelled the people of the land to follow his holiness reforms.

"Making" someone worship sounds like a violation of conscience to my Baptist ears. And I've never "torn my clothes" in response to a divine directive. But Josiah is showing us something about leadership. There is a time to keep a cool head as a leader. There is a season to build consensus and wait for followers to arrive at their own conclusions. But once in a great while, when the urgency and gravity of a situation demands it, there is a time for a leader to have an emotional demonstration of personal affectedness, and a season to be quite directive in compelling followers to come along.

Overplaying the emotional and directive style makes a leader a dictator. But never using it can stand in the way of reforms that will not otherwise happen.

John P. Chandler

EZRA 4

LEADING THROUGH OPPOSITION

"Then the people of the land discouraged the people of Judah, and made them afraid to build, and they bribed officials to frustrate their plan ..." – **Ezra 4:4-5**

The book of Ezra recounts the work of God's people to rebuild a destroyed temple and city in Jerusalem after Babylonian Exile. It is like a retelling of the Exodus story, meant to point out God's provision to deliver his people so that they could resume the life of worship that would make them a witness to the world.

Interestingly, much of the story concerns the resistance God's people encounter while doing this good and worthy work. There is little discussion of the motives for opposition and much discussion of tactics, which include slander, innuendo, exaggeration, rumor, pandering to fears, appealing to baser military and combative instincts, and rewriting history. These tactics occupy large portions of the book of Ezra (and its companion book, Nehemiah). Why would the story devote such attention to the opposition of rebuilding?

One, because it is true! Every leader and every noble cause will face and must overcome this sort of (often unfair) resistance.

Two, because much of the purpose of the story has to do with the people of God learning how to be chosen without the propping up of a monarch and when things are demanding. No sugar daddy is going to take care of this work, and it isn't going to be easy. The people have to buckle up and do the work.

Every wise leader prepares his or her people for sailing in rough waters. For what we learn to do in extremes and in the face of opposition forges us for the work that needs to be done.

Prayer: *Lord, let me never deceive the people I lead into believing that our common task is easy. Let me instead steel their courage and determination to the hard, good thing. In the name of the Lord Jesus who was willing to do the hard, good thing and win salvation for all through the cross, Amen.*

John P. Chandler

195

EZRA 10

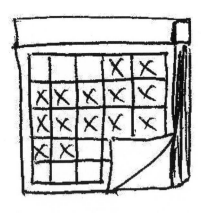

NOT A TASK
FOR A DAY OR TWO

"It is so; we must do as you have said. But the people are
many, and it is a time of heavy rain; we cannot stand in the
open. Nor is this a task for one day or for two, for many of us
have transgressed in this matter." – Ezra 10:12-13

As he led the people of God to rebuild temple and city, Ezra got in touch with the depth of the work to be done, and the shortcomings that led to the crisis in the first place. He is almost immobilized with grief and regret, but does the difficult work of announcing the hard relational work that the people must do (extracting themselves from wrongful alliances). Even harder, Ezra doesn't impose his will as a leader on the people but lets them own the task for themselves: "It is so; we must do as you have said."

Real wisdom, though, comes in the subsequent exchange. The people, while willing, are overwhelmed by the enormity of the task and ask for time to work it out: "Nor is this a task for a day or two," they say. Ezra listens and works with them for a slow, thorough, systemic response. And by the end of the book, the difficult work is done.

Most leaders overestimate what they can get done in one year and underestimate what they can get done in ten years. Wise leaders know when to push a radical agenda but allow it appropriate time to be worked out incrementally.

NEHEMIAH 2

"You see the trouble we are in, how Jerusalem lies in ruins with its gates burned. Come, let us rebuild the wall of Jerusalem ..." – **Nehemiah 2:17**

Having heard (and preached) through Nehemiah for church building campaigns to the point of being tiresome, I received a fresh perspective on rebuilding a ruined city while visiting Christchurch, New Zealand after its earthquakes. To watch ordinary Baptist people respond steadily, persistently, diligently – there is little that is flashy and spectacular in such leadership, but it is a parable about leadership nonetheless.

The books of Ezra and Nehemiah were originally one book. While Ezra was a schooled clergyman, Nehemiah was not. It showed. Nehemiah's prayers are unpolished and straightforward, and he is not above using rough means to reach his goals. Yet, he was a man of action who leveraged his relational capital and life skills to lead in the rebuilding of a city.

It takes both types of leaders and a partnership and valuing between them. Most great leadership, in fact, occurs in pairs and teams. Those who (like Ezra) are in official positions of leadership would do well to identify, deploy, and value leaders on the field (like Nehemiah) who do the leg work of rebuilding broken communities and nations.

Exercise: *Who are your companion leaders? Name two or three people whose strengths are different but complementary to yours. Then list a few ways you can leverage the strengths of these ordinary partners for extraordinary benefit.*

NEHEMIAH 5

"Now there was a great outcry of the people and of their wives against their Jewish kin." – **Nehemiah 5:1**

Nehemiah was a task-oriented leader who helped the broken people of Jerusalem rebuild their broken city. He led them to build the modern equivalent of a coliseum very quickly. After ninety years of languishing, they steamrolled through this project in fifty-two days!

The project met with opposition from all sides:

- North (Sanballat and the Samaritans);

- East (Tobiah and the Ammonites);

- South (Geshom and the Arabs); and

- West (the Ashdodites or Philistines).

However, in chapter 5, we see that the project was also challenged internally. There is a *"great outcry of the people and of their wives against their Jewish kin"* (v. 1). Internal tensions threaten to derail the work. Nehemiah responds in two significant ways:

1. He listens even to the "wives" – rare in that day and culture!; and

2. "Neither I nor my brothers ate the food allowance of the governor" (v. 14). When people were starving, the leader modeled austerity.

Task-oriented leaders always remember that they are leading human beings. They are willing listen to interruptions to the task. And they participate in the solutions to which they point.

NEHEMIAH 6

"Sanballat and Geshem sent to me, saying, "Come let us meet together in one of the villages in the plain of Ono. But they intended to do me harm." – Nehemiah 6:2

Nehemiah is a man of action, called by God to repair the wall of Jerusalem and rebuild the city. It is a noble task. But sometimes noble tasks threaten the interests of others, and Nehemiah, for all of his attempts to do this work, attracts enemies. Two of them, Sanballat and Geshem, think Nehemiah is getting too big for his britches, and they accuse him of treason.

These opponents try various threats – intimidation, extortion, tattling. But in Nehemiah 6, they attempt perhaps the most common and insidious threat to leaders: distraction. Nehemiah wants to work; his opponents want to talk. Granted, sometimes negotiation and diplomacy is part of the work. But often, it is little more than procrastination, a failure to move, and the paralysis of analysis.

Nehemiah refuses to grant an audience with these distractors. They are persistent, hoping to wear him down. But he says, "*Why should the work stop while I leave it to come to you?*" (v. 3).

In that is a lesson for leaders: there may be a time to discuss and negotiate. But there is also a time for action, and to delay at that point is to fail to work and fail to lead.

NEHEMIAH 7

DEALING WITH TACTICS OF OPPONENTS

"Then I sent to him, saying, "No such things as you say have been done; you are inventing them out of your own mind" – for they all wanted to frighten us, thinking, "Their hands will drop from the work, and it will not be done." But now, O God, strengthen my hands." – Nehemiah 6:8-9

Against long odds and with diligence and persistence, Nehemiah has led the people of God to a point where they have nearly completed the great project of rebuilding the walls of the city. Early on, his opponents could rely on prevailing social pessimism to discourage this work. But now, the finish line is in sight, and Nehemiah's opponents change tactics in order to step up their attack. Now the attack gets personal. Failing to malign the project, Tobiah and Sanballat now go after Nehemiah himself. They slander his:

> relationship with the king,

> relationship with God, and

> relationship with the city.

In short, character assassination accuses a leader of treason, bad faith, and self-interest. Many a leader makes the mistake of returning personal attack in kind, or with defensiveness. But Nehemiah models a wiser way. Refusing to answer his opponents point by point, he instead prays for God's strength and resolve. Wise leaders refuse to play by deceitful rules of engagement set by adversaries. They counter with open, frank statements that counter bluffs, discern traps, and refuse to be intimidated. And they rely on God's strength for their own!

NEHEMIAH 8

HEAD DOWN, HANDS UP

"Then Ezra blessed the Lord, the great God, and all the people answered, Amen, Amen," lifting up their hands. Then they bowed their heads and worshiped the Lord with their faces to the ground." **– Nehemiah 8:6**

Having led the people to complete the rebuilt wall around Jerusalem, Nehemiah now partners with the scribe, Ezra, in a new leadership arrangement. It is not enough to rebuild the wall; the people themselves also need rebuilding.

They are hungry for it and the summon Ezra to teach them the Law. A six-hour sermon (!) reconnects God's people with their identity as worshipers and givers. They re-enact the Feast of Booths to remember to trust God, not their own walls and defenses. It is a second Exodus, a new liberation. The people don't want to be bossed, but they do seek guidance, the moral compass of the ways of God.

The posture of the people is deeply symbolic: bowed hands and lifted hands. This is a picture of the redeemed society toward which we lead: a humble, devoted, and teachable people ("*bowed heads*"), manifested in how they learn, worship, serve, give, and celebrate ("*lifting hands*"). This is the vision of a society toward which we want to lead: heads down in work, hand up in humility and gratitude.

NEHEMIAH 13

BUILDING PEOPLE

"Thus I cleansed them from everything foreign, and I established the duties of the priests and Levites, each in his work ...." – Nehemiah 13:30

The book of Nehemiah ends with an account of this great leader having to lead the people all the way to the end. He is most remembered for helping the returning exiles rebuild the wall around Jerusalem in only fifty-two days and in the face of great opposition. But his work with the recalcitrant, backsliding people continues after the wall is built, because the people of the city continue to slip.

In the newly re-established Jerusalem, the people continue to work on the Sabbath and inter-marry with spiritual foreigners, and so Nehemiah has to re-establish holy time and holy space. He threatens, cajoles, and even violently confronts those who violate. The one who has been so patient in building the wall is now impatient with those who threaten the identity of the community. Verse 25 says, *"I contended with them and cursed them and beat some of them and pulled out their hair"* – wow! It is ongoing, never-finished work. Jesus would deal with the same issues almost five hundred years later. Pastors deal with it today.

That's because building people is harder than building projects. And the real work of the leader is more difficult to measure than the establishment of bricks and mortar. It is about helping people establish good work, the right relationships, and a rhythm of life that is in keeping with the good of the community. The best leaders build people.

ESTHER 1

"Drinking was by flagons, without restraint: for the king had given orders to all the officials of the palace to do as each one desired." – Esther 1:8

The story of Esther is told by the Jewish people during the festival of Purim. Full of irony and comedy, it is often criticized for not being "religious" enough to be included in the Bible. But the careful reader will find in it plenty of examples – positive and negative – of how to lead and live as a minority within a compromised land. The twin dangers facing the people of God in that day (in most days, actually) are <u>elimination</u> and <u>assimilation</u>. There is as much danger in giving in and becoming indistinct from the wider society as there is in facing persecution from it, and the wise (like Esther) learn to negotiate a middle place.

One negative example of an accommodated leader is king Ahasuerus. He is presented as a buffoon, but a dangerous one. His opening act is to host a 180-day feast for the entire empire *"from India to Ethiopia"* (v. 1). That wasn't enough (!), so it's followed by a seven-day drinking fest (vv. 5-7). It is all done *"without restraint"* (v. 8). Because he is unaccustomed to nuance, when the king faces a single slight, he is easily led into ordering a pogrom.

We learn first thing that negative leadership is marked by lack of <u>proportion</u>. Just because you have abundance at your disposal doesn't mean you squander it. Unlike Ahasuerus, wise leaders know modesty, nuance, and diplomatic middle ways. The antidote to lack of proportion is a sense of *propriety*. Leaders know the "proper" (proportionate) response.

Prayer: *Lord of all, grant to me today a sense of proportion. Make me wise over whatever I rule. And when I am in the minority, show me how to navigate so that I am neither discounted nor compromised beyond distinction. In the name of Jesus, who was both powerful and humble, Amen.*

John P. Chandler

ESTHER 3

CONSEQUENCES
OF BAD ADVISORS

*"The king said to Haman, "The money is given to you, and
the people as well, to do with them as it seems good to you."*
– Esther 3:11

Praying the Kings

Ahaseurus, king of the Persian empire, has already been exposed as a poor leader. He may lead one hundred twenty-seven provinces *"from India to Ethiopia"* (Esther 1:1), but his opening scene in the book is one of drunken excess. He has no sense of "proportion" as a leader. He is rash, impulsive – and (unfortunately) quite powerful.

In chapter 3, he picks the wrong chief of staff. After an episode in chapter 2, we expected Mordecai to be named to a high post of leadership. But while Mordecai had done the nation and king a great behind-the-scenes service in uncovering an assassination plot, he is overlooked. The king instead selects Haman to lead. Why? We soon see that Haman is as vain and rash as the king himself. Sometimes leaders dangerously pick people in their own mirror image.

Haman's first act of national leadership is to order not only the elimination of his rival Mordecai but the extermination of Mordecai's entire race in a pogrom. Haman easily (mis)leads the king, and with great efficiency, via the famous Persian postal system, and orders for genocide are sent to be carried out empire-wide. Haman and Ahaseurus end a long work day by sitting down for a drink. Meanwhile the city is *"thrown into confusion"* (v. 15).

Unwise leaders pick advisors with agendas and listen to them uncritically. The dangerous consequences are that the wrong aims are carried out with startling efficiency.

John P. Chandler 213

ESTHER 4

"The king said to her, "What is it, Queen Esther? What is your request? It shall be given to you, even to half of my kingdom." Then Esther said, "If it pleases the king, let the king and Haman come today to a banquet that I have prepared for the king." **– Esther 5:3-4**

Like any well-told story, the book of Esther is full of characters whose traits illuminate. Most royal characters in the story come across as disproportionately reactive. This impulsivity, when combined with their great power and influence, is dangerous. It makes leaders like king Ahaseurus and his royal henchman Haman capable of ordering genocide as part of a day's work.

In contrast, Esther is a model of restraint. She takes great risk in approaching the king unbidden. But he favors her and even grants her the opening to request a big favor. She knows what she wants (the salvation of her own Jewish people) but, in holding back from asking for it right away, demonstrates a great leadership principle. Namely, in a time of rash decision-making, she shows instead:

1. Restraint, and

2. Investment in relational good-will.

Good leaders are not simply opportunistic to pounce on any small opening in any conversation to further their own ends. They instead build "relational capital" in an ongoing manner. Thus, over time, they strengthen the human bonds that make the difficult conversations down the road possible.

ESTHER 7-10

EGO-FREE LEADERSHIP

*"... The king again said to Esther, "What is your petition,
Queen Esther? It shall be granted you. And what is your
request? Even to the half of my kingdom, it shall be fulfilled."
Then Queen Esther answered, "If I have won your favor, O
king, and if it pleases the king, let my life be given me – that
is my petition – and the lives of my people – that is my
request." – Esther 7:2-3*

The story of Esther is a happy tale of a good outcome in a perilous situation. What began as potential genocide through the duping of an unscrupulous advisor ends with Mordecai (Esther's Jewish uncle) reigning happily alongside of a foreign king: *"... and he was powerful among the Jews and popular with his many kindred, for he sought the good of his people and interceded for the welfare of all his descendants"* (10:3). It is an ideal picture of godly leadership within an accommodated culture.

The success story hinges on the work of Esther, who is placed in a position of responsibility by a God whose name is never mentioned, but who is working in circumstances and in people throughout. Esther's uncle Mordecai voices to her the most famous words of the book, *"Who knows? Perhaps you have come to royal dignity for just such a time as this"* (Esther 4:14)

She is up to the task because she is fundamentally interested more in the welfare of her people than in her own aggrandizement or accumulation. When asked for anything she wants, she requests *"the lives of my people."* This is Solomon-like wisdom! It is made all-the-more striking in contrast with the scheming Haman, whose towering ego is symbolized by the fifty-cubit-high gallows on which he intended to hang Esther. Ironically, he himself is hanged on them, hoisted by the excesses of his own ego and ambition.

Perhaps Esther showed little ego as a leader because she was a female foreigner at risk by a powerful enemy, advising uncle, and easily-fooled king. But perhaps her ego-free leadership is instead the moral of the story – and the trait Israel learned to celebrate, and that wise people since then have learned to follow.

John P. Chandler   217

Acknowledgements

Time and space are the media through which God creates, and through which we create. I would like to thank the dear people who have given gifts of time and space for writing this book. The beloved community they offer to me is a sign of the in-breaking Kingdom of God!

It is a joy to be enfolded within the world Baptist family, and John Upton symbolizes to me everything I love about my tribe: a global and Kingdom perspective, highly relational, and likeable, effective leadership. He is not only President of the Baptist World Alliance and Executive Director for Virginia Baptists, but the best boss I have ever had or seen! Thanks to John and to all of my friends and colleagues in the Baptist General Association of Virginia for the blessing and encouragement to work on this project. A shout-out to all in the "Uptick" tribe who are "winning the first battle of the day" and "working from rest." Thanks to David Bailey for creative and concrete conversation. Special thanks to dear friends and strategic collaborators Jim Baucom and Laura McDaniel – your vision, laughter, and partnership mean the world to me.

Thanks for the gifts of friends in the Argentina Baptist Association, especially Daniel Carro, Andrés Forteza and Paula Rodriguez (and Enzo), Daniel Lafortiva and Lili Mazzoni, Gustavo Moccia, Esteban and Mariella Licatta, Raúl Scialabba, and Sonia Trivillin, a God-gifted teacher and translator.

Thanks also to Joshua DuBois, formerly of the White House's

Office of Faith-based and Neighborhood Partnerships, for spurring the project and demonstrating collaborative leadership. Thanks to Mike Breen, Steve Cockram, and all of the 3DM *oikos* for friendship, invitation/challenge, huddles, and for teaching the value of LifeShapes as a tool for discipleship. Thanks to my awesome community of faith, All Souls Charlottesville, especially to Jessica Luttrull for using God's gift of your art.

Finally, thanks to my sons, Preston and Roland, not only for Spanish inspiration, but for becoming great young spiritual leaders. (Mingo, you too!) And saving the best for last, thanks to the love of my life, Mary, for the idea to start this work, for the quiet time and space every morning to help me practice what I preach, and for the example of how to listen and respond to God with a generous heart.

"I thank my God every time I remember you, constantly praying with joy in every one of my prayers for all of you, because of your sharing in the gospel from the first day until now. I am confident of this, that the one who began a good work among you will bring it to completion by the day of Jesus Christ." – Philippians 1:3-6

Selected Bibliography

All Scripture quotes are from the New Revised Standard Version.

Note: In some instances, I have included a quote or idea from someone by name without citing a specific source. When no source is cited, this indicates one of several possible situations: that

1. the quote or idea was cited within a commentary of another author listed below on that particular biblical passage, or

2. I heard it from them first hand in a personal conversation or sermon, or

3. I heard it attributed to them second hand orally in a lecture or conversation.

I have done this in an order to reduce footnoting distractions or when I am uncertain of the original source. I hope readers will appreciate this intent. Authors, speakers, and historical citations are noted in the index.

Bechtel, Carol M. *Esther,* Interpretation: A Bible Commentary for Teaching and Preaching, John Knox Press, Atlanta, GA, 2002.

Blenkinsopp, Joseph. *Ezra-Nehemiah,* Old Testament Library, translated by Herbert Hartwell, The Westminster Press, Philadelphia, PA, 1988.

Breen, Mike. *Covenant and Kingdom: The DNA of the Bible,* 3DMinistries, Pawleys Island SC, 2011.

___ and Steve Cockram. *Building a Discipling Culture: How to Release a Missional Movement by Discipling People Like Jesus Did,* 3DMinistries, Pawleys Island, SC, 2011.

Brueggemann, Walter. *1 Kings,* Knox Preaching Guides, John Knox Press, Atlanta, GA, 1982.

___. *2 Kings,* Knox Preaching Guides, John Knox Press, Atlanta, GA, 1982.

___. *First and Second Samuel,* Interpretation: A Bible Commentary for Teaching and Preaching, John Knox Press, Atlanta, GA, 1990.

Claypool, John. *Tracks of a Fellow Struggler: Living and Growing Through Grief,* Morehouse Publishing, Harrisburg, PA, 2004.

Coggins, Richard J., and S. Paul Re'emi. *Nahum, Obadiah, Esther: Israel among the Nations,* International Theological Commentary, Wm. B. Eerdmans Publishing Company, Grand Rapids, MI, 1985.

Creach, Jerome F. D. *Joshua,* Interpretation: A Bible Commentary for Teaching and Preaching, John Knox Press, Atlanta, GA, 2003.

Foster, Richard, and Dallas Willard, Walter Brueggemann. *The Life with God Bible,* HarperCollins, New York, NY, 1989.

Gladwell, Malcolm. *Blink: The Power of Thinking Without Thinking,* Little, Brown, and Company, Time Warner Book Group, New York, NY, 2005.

Hamlin, E. John. *Joshua: Inheriting the Land*, International Theological Commentary, Wm. B. Eerdmans Publishing Company, Grand Rapids, MI, 1983.

___. *Judges: At Risk in the Promised Land*, International Theological Commentary, Wm. B. Eerdmans Publishing Company, Grand Rapids, MI, 1990.

Nelson, Richard. *First and Second Kings,* Interpretation series, John Knox Press, Atlanta, GA, 1987.

Newsome, James D., Jr. *1 Samuel/2 Samuel,* Knox Preaching Guides, John Knox Press, Atlanta, GA, 1982.

Niebuhr, H. Richard. *Christ and Culture,* Harper and Row, New York, NY, 1951.

Peterson, Eugene. *Five Smooth Stones for Pastoral Work,* Eerdmans, Grand Rapids, MI, 1980.

Rath, Tom. *Vital Friends: The People You Can't Afford to Live Without,* Gallup Press, Princeton, NJ, 2006.

Rice, Gene. *1 Kings: Nations under God,* International Theological Commentary, Wm. B. Eerdmans Publishing Company, Grand Rapids, MI, 1990.

Roam, Dan. *The Back of the Napkin (Expanded Edition): Solving Problems and Selling Ideas with Pictures,* Penguin Group, New York, NY, 2009.

Sakenfeld, Katharine Doob. *Ruth,* Interpretation series, John Knox Press, Atlanta, GA, 1999.

Throntveit, Mark A. *Ezra-Nehemiah,* Interpretation: A Bible Commentary for Teaching and Preaching, John Knox Press, Atlanta, GA, 1992.

Tillich, Paul. *Systematic Theology: Three Volumes in One,* University Of Chicago Press 1st edition, Chicago, IL, 1967.

Tuell, Steven S. *First and Second Chronicles,* Interpretation: A Bible Commentary for Teaching and Preaching, John Knox Press, Atlanta, GA, 2001.

Tufte, Edward R. *Beautiful Evidence,* Graphics Press, first edition July 2006.

____. *Envisioning Information,* Graphics Press, 1990.

____. *Visual Explanations: Images and Quantities, Evidence and Narrative,* Graphics Press, 1997.

Willard, Dallas. *Hearing God Through the Year (Through the Year Devotionals),* IVP Books, 2004.

___. *Hearing God, Updated and Expanded: Developing a Conversational Relationship with God,* IVP Books, 2012.

___. *The Spirit of the Disciplines: Understanding How God Changes Lives,* HarperOne, 1990.

___. *In Search of Guidance: Developing a Conversational Relationship with God,* HarperCollins, 1993.

Table of Scripture Chapters

Joshua 1, 2, 3, 5, 7, 10, 14, 17, 20-22, 23, 24 (11 devotions total included)

Judges 1, 3, 4-5, 7, 8, 9, 11, 13-16, 21 (9)

Ruth 1, 3-4 (2)

1 Samuel 1, 3, 8, 14, 15, 16-17, 20, 28, 30 (9)

2 Samuel 2, 3, 6, 11, 14, 15, 17, 18, 23 (9)

1 Kings 3, 4, 5, 9, 10, 12, 13, 14, 17, 18, 19, 21,22 (13)

2 Kings 1, 2, 3, 4, 5, 6, 7, 9, 12, 13, 16, 17, 18, 20, 21, 22, 23 (17)

1 Chronicles 13, 15, 17, 21, 27, 29 (6)

2 Chronicles 2, 5-6, 15, 21-23, 24, 25, 26, 28, 30, 33, 34 (11)

Ezra 4, 10 (2)

Nehemiah 2, 5, 6, 7, 8, 13 (6)

Esther 1, 3, 4, 7-10 (4)

Index